CRAFT, COST & CALL

How to Build a Life as a Christian Writer

By Patricia Paddey and Karen Stiller

◆ FriesenPress

Suite 300 - 990 Fort St
Victoria, BC, V8V 3K2
Canada

www.friesenpress.com

Illustrated by Jenna Paddey

Scriptures marked KJV are taken from the KING JAMES VERSION
(KJV): KING JAMES VERSION, public domain.

ISBN
978-1-5255-5411-7 (Hardcover)
978-1-5255-5412-4 (Paperback)
978-1-5255-5413-1 (eBook)

1. *Language Arts & Disciplines, Composition & Creative Writing,
Nonfiction (incl. Memoirs)*

Distributed to the trade by The Ingram Book Company

ENDORSEMENTS

Written with generosity and contagious zest, this book combines inspiration, information, and reflection on the writing life by two Canadian writers who have established careers as standard-bearers for excellence in Christian writing. Their honest sharing will encourage and enable writers who are aspiring or just plain weary to press on with diligence, discipline, and so experience the joy of the gift of words.
– Maxine Hancock, Author of *Gold from the Fire: Postcards from a Prairie Pilgrimage,* Professor Emerita, Interdisciplinary Studies and Spiritual Theology, Regent College.

This book—it's like I found a bundle of money in a paper bag under a park bench. I'm leaping for joy and feeling a tad guilty all at once. I have been writing for print for a goodly while, and every word of this little masterpiece has me either nodding, sagely, my approval or wincing, ashamedly, at things I once knew and then forgot, or maybe never knew at all. Karen Stiller and Patricia Paddey stuff these few pages with so much wit, wisdom, clear prose, and hard-earned

counsel that no writer—no matter how green or seasoned—will fail to benefit from it. Take the money and run.
– Mark Buchanan, Author of *God Speed: Walking as Spiritual Practice,* Associate Professor of Pastoral Theology at Ambrose University.

Finally, writers of faith have a relevant, tactful, and informative survival guide in *Craft, Cost & Call.* Together, Patricia Paddey and Karen Stiller offer a wealth of shared experience in creating a meaningful writing life while navigating distractions, financial realities, and performance pressures in a newly changing publication landscape.
– Carolyn A. Weber, Author of *Surprised by Oxford,* Associate Professor of Literature, Heritage College & Seminary, and Brescia University College.

Craft, Cost & Call is a concise, easy-to-read introduction to nonfiction writing for people considering it as a career, although it would also be a great gift for someone who thinks of it as a hobby. The authors share their Christian perspectives and career experiences with diverse genres of writing in a frank, friendly, and affirming way. There's lots of great, practical advice, either drawing on personal (and embarrassing) anecdotes or memorable quotes from accomplished mainstream writers. Writers can never afford to stop learning, and this book will help many along that journey.
– Bill Fledderus, Senior Editor, *Faith Today* magazine, and Adjunct Lecturer/Journalism Instructor, Redeemer University College.

I've worked with both Patricia Paddey and Karen Stiller over several years, and I've gotten to know their work. Both of them are excellent writers, and I turn to them frequently when I need something written on a tight deadline for my unique audience. I'm grateful to know them as colleagues in the world of writing.

I'm grateful to Paddey and Stiller for this book, which is chock-full of help for writers of all kinds. I love the earthy wisdom and encouraging (and sometimes sobering) anecdotes of success and failure. This is not a book designed to sell you anything. Rather, read it, savor it, and decide what applies to your circumstances. You'll probably find, as I did, that you keep mulling it over long after you put it down.
– Jay Blossom, Publisher, *In Trust* magazine, In Trust Center for Theological Schools.

In *Craft, Cost & Call,* Stiller and Paddey offer a feast of writing advice as delicious as it is nourishing. Practical, wise, and enormously helpful, this book manifests the beautiful writing it aims to inspire (and offers a few belly laughs to boot). I finished the book longing to be a better writer, and newly equipped to move in that direction. I'll be ordering copies for all my writer friends.
-Carolyn Arends, Recording Artist and Renovaré Director of Education.

DEDICATION

To all those writers who have inspired and taught us. Thank you.

TABLE OF CONTENTS

INTRODUCTION

If we could have you to ourselves for an afternoon in a cottage with a view of the lake, we would pour you a mug of tea, hand you a butter tart from that tiny bakery just outside of town, and tell you everything we know about building a life as a Christian writer.

Our writing careers have spanned twenty years or more, and one constant for both of us—besides all the practicing, failing, succeeding, trying again and again, being published, and not being published—has been our desire to learn more and be better, and the fact that we have always learned from other writers.

This book represents all that we know so far about good writing and how to make it as a professional writer. Even if writing is a sideline for you, or a hobby, you will find tips and insights here to improve your writing and increase your chance of being published—if being published is your goal.

This book is our conversation with you about what we have learned through success and failure.

We have divided the book into three main sections, areas we consider to be vital to the writing life: Craft, Cost, & Call. Craft is, of course, the how-to of writing. We have poured out for you tips, insights, lessons, and the shortcuts and long roads of writing, as we know them to be true.

You will learn how to conduct interviews without making a fool of yourself, how to construct an outline for an article, and then how to see your work clearly enough to make it better.

Cost covers the mechanics of your business, including things like setting up an office, and the nitty gritty bits like how to prepare an invoice, what to charge, and of course, how to keep improving as a writer. This section is extremely practical, and something writers don't often speak about to each other. Talking over these topics with one another over the years has helped us to not only do business better, but to build better writing lives.

Finally, Call considers what it means to be a writer who is also a person of faith, because that is who we are and it has mattered.

We have included some true stories throughout the book, which document our own experiences wrestling these writing lessons into our lives, and which offer you glimpses of "A Writer's Life." There are moments that gave us joy and others that made us cringe and want to curl up and hide for a while. If you are a writer, you will have both of those kinds of moments. That is for certain.

We also offer suggestions for exercises and techniques you might like to try. We promise: there is value in working through them. They will strengthen your courage and develop your craft. You need both courage and craft as you test out your writing wings.

We are two friends who have encouraged each other along, written books together, shared writing contracts, and made it work to be professional writers in a time when that might feel difficult to do.

It *is* hard work to be a writer. That is the first thing we would tell you. But it is worth it. And it is possible even to make a living being a writer. It is definitely possible to improve as a writer, wherever you are on the writing journey today.

You may not be trying to carve out a career as a writer, but you may consider writing to be a part of your calling. It is something you do because you love it, and you want to be better at it and you feel that God has beckoned you to this ancient craft and calling.

The desire to improve is a good and God-honoring thing.

In 1 Peter 4:10–11, the apostle writes that each one of us must use "the special gift" we have received from God for the good of others, so that in all things God will be praised. We do consider writing a gift, and whether we've been writing books or blogs, ads or articles, it is a gift we have sought to share so that others might learn and be blessed.

So on the following pages we have condensed all we know—so far—about what makes writing good and what makes the writing life great, and we offer it here for you. (This book is the beginning of the conversation. Join us on the CraftCostCall Facebook page for even more or visit CraftCostCall.com.)

And now, let us tell you what we know.

CRAFT

"Bringing order and beauty out of disorder and chaos, and meaning out of the meanest of circumstances, is God-work, in which we may be co-creators."

– Luci Shaw, "Beauty and the Creative Impulse" in
The Christian Imagination

What is good writing?

You know it when you read it. Good writing is clean and uncluttered, like a beautiful room in a lovely home. Good writing does not confuse or mislead, or show off. Good writing is content with simple words, such as daisy and jug. It doesn't try to impress with its words, but with its thinking. Good writing comes from time spent and clear notes, and maybe even a plan, although not always.

Good writing comes from setting fear aside and just getting started, even when you don't want to. Good writing comes after you walk the dog, pace the room, avoid even glancing at your laptop, call a friend, wring your hands, and watch Netflix. Good writing comes from just getting it out and thinking it is magnificent. You leave it alone because it is complete and ready and then return to it in a day or two and see it for the miserable mess that it is. You wonder who broke in and stole your masterpiece.

But do not despair. It can be fixed, and that process of fixing it is what truly makes good writing. You can tear your writing apart and put it back together again, and you must do that.

Here is the terrible news of good writing: it takes so much time and effort. It is so much work.

It rarely and most likely never happens on the first or even the fourth try. Good writing can come from a natural gift, just like someone who is born graceful and lithe might eventually become a ballerina or an acrobat. But they must try. There is no strolling into the show or the circus or onto the stage without first spending hours in rehearsal. Here is the good news of good writing: these skills can be taught and learned and practiced until your page does come alive for you and also for the reader you are trying to reach or touch or move.

In his wonderful book *On Writing: A Memoir of the Craft,* Stephen King writes that "… it is possible, with lots of hard work, dedication, and timely help, to make a good writer out of a merely competent one." What do you think of that? It is hopeful, isn't it? We left out the first part of the quote where King says that bad writers do exist, and not a lot can be done for them, but you should look that up yourself. Most of us start out competent and then we can become good, maybe even very good.

Good writing comes from a deep desire and a burning fire in the belly to make it as a writer. It is not enough to be inspired—we must be instructed. We must become good enough at our craft to create good enough writing, and then move beyond good enough to excellence.

Good writing is hard work. And yes, it is also joy.

Try this:

Think of a veteran writer you could approach and ask to meet with you. Buy them lunch or coffee, or interview them over the phone. Ask them about their writing journey and what advice they might offer to a new writer. Send them an email or hand-written note afterward, thanking them for their time and willingness to share their insights with you. They will remember you.

A Writer's Life
Encouragement

I sat beside an older gentleman on a plane once who was making careful notes in a red spiral notebook. Because I'm nosey, and I thought maybe he was a writer, I asked him what he was doing.

He told me he was sketching out plans for an upcoming sailing trip he was taking from Florida, a very long list of things to check and double-check before he set sail for the Bahamas. But as it turns out, he was a writer too. He told me about the short story collection of incredible but true stories he had independently published recently.

He asked what I did for a living, and I told him that I, too, was a writer. He said he had thought this when I first sat down. I was pleased. Maybe I exuded a hip writer vibe after all with my cat eyeglasses and careless bohemian chic (crumpled look)?

But no.

He assumed I was a writer because I was carrying illustrations from a museum I had visited. He thought they were the pictures from the children's book I'm not writing. I told him what kind of a writer I really am and we talked for the entire flight home.

He shared his discouragement at the difficulties of finding agents and publishers. I suggested he join a writers' group for support and encouragement.

He recounted the scene from *Midnight in Paris* when Ernest Hemingway tells Owen Wilson to avoid other writers because they are so competitive. I handed him the "Humans Write" pen I had also bought at the gift shop and told him I wanted him to have it.

When I returned from the teeny tiny washroom at the back of the plane, my new friend had dug out his favorite pen to give to me. And so we departed, row mates and fellow writers, just a little bit encouraged, each of us with a new pen. – KS

Read well and widely

One wonderful thing about learning to write well is that you can do it partly by reading well, and by that we mean reading widely. If you want to write, you must read. You can't say this about every craft or vocation: you don't become excellent as a plumber by turning a tap on and off or just enjoying a tall, cool glass of water and gazing at the sink. But you can become a better writer by reading. This is extremely fortunate for writers. It is a true bonus.

Marilyn Chandler McEntyre describes learning to read as "a lifelong process." In her thought-provoking book *Caring for Words in a Culture of Lies*, Chandler McEntyre explains, "What we learned in first grade or fifth, or in our first encounter with Steinbeck or Spenser or the *New York Times,* has layered and refined our reading sensibilities and strategies ... If we continue to seek out worthwhile writers, we find that each one of them has something to teach us about how to read."

Writers read for our souls, yes, but also for our strategy. We absolutely must read the publications in which we want our writing to appear.

Get acquainted with those publications from the front cover to the back. Wander around inside them and read even the articles that don't instantly attract you. Ask yourself: Why was this topic chosen and this article written? Think about what you are reading. Why is it working or not working? What is the writer *doing*? Get a sense of the topics or issues the publication routinely covers and set your mind in that direction.

Purposefully read the kinds of books you want to write. This is reading that is both mindful and mercenary, intentional and inspiring.

Pay attention to who and what wins writing awards each year, and read those articles and those books. An award is not an absolute guarantee of greatness of course, but it comes close. We've all viewed at least one painting in a gallery and thought, "Why … I could have painted that." Well, of course we could not have painted that! We know the truth. The same thing can happen with an award-winning book or article. Don't feel competitive with it; this is not a swim meet. Let it inspire you.

Read great books. Devour them. Often.

There is something magical that can happen when you read great writing as a writer. After a time, you may feel a shift inside your stomach, a kind of leap of optimism and energy that if you only had a notebook and pen, or if your laptop was charged and open in front of you, something great would happen. A window has opened, and you can climb through it and get somewhere new. If we only surfed, which we do not, we think this might be what it's like as you lie on your board and then suddenly are on top of a wave, riding it to shore. Someone else's beautiful writing, the lyrical and lovely parts, can inspire you to write very well, at that exact moment. Grab your notebook and seize that moment. Dani Shapiro in her beautiful book *Still Writing: The Perils and Pleasures of a Creative Life* writes: "Fill your ears with the music of good sentences, and when you finally approach the page yourself, that music will carry you."

You might even choose to have a small selection of great writing on your desk. Each morning you dip into a beautiful poem or a startling paragraph or two from a great book you love and this, like eating a bowl of steel cut oats for breakfast, can fill you up and at least point you in the best direction for the day.

In *The Art of Memoir*, author Mary Karr advises writers to read the classics and other good books from earlier times. "Reading through history cultivates in a writer a standard of quality higher than the marketplace," she writes. "You can be a slave to current magazines or a slave to history. History's harder, but also more stable—and the books are better because they've been culled over time."

This insight about reading is one of the three pieces of advice Karr says she has heard consistently through the years from other writers. What are the other two? "(1) Writing is painful—it's 'fun' only for novices, the very young, and hacks; (2) other than a few instances of good luck, good work *only* comes through revision." We quote Karr because she is a brilliant writer and because we completely agree with that advice, and also because she has written so richly about writing, and that is the other kind of reading writers can do: read about writing. There are so many excellent writing books out there. Do read them, but please promise that you won't spend years just reading about writing. At some point to be a writer, you must actually write.

Dani Shapiro says that "Reading great work is exhilarating. It shows us what is possible." And C.S. Lewis famously said we read to know we are not alone. And so that must mean we write to remind others that they are not alone either.

Try this:

Visit a large book store or library and browse their magazine section or new book releases. In the magazines, take note of the kinds of articles that are being published, and their topics. In the book section, what is being prominently displayed? What books are on the shelves in the genres in which you want to write? What can you learn from what you observe?

A Writer's Life
Words

One weekend I sat at my dining room table and consumed a pie recipe. It was almost a poem, especially when I reached this line: "Tumble in the cranberries." That was the moment I realized even a recipe can be beautifully written. Good writing can be anywhere.

Because that is exactly what cranberries do, as anyone who has ever made cranberry sauce can tell you. They tumble. They are so fat and firm at the same time, they have no choice. They are berries packed so full of themselves in their tight little red skins that they bounce off of each other into the pot … or the pie.

I loved this recipe that I will never, ever make. I cannot imagine ever having the time or the patience to individually rub each pea-sized piece of butter between my thumb and finger, flattening them into little discs that will help make the best pastry ever.

My pie, I know, would not turn out as if it had been made by poem. But just being reminded of the richness of words, and how with just the smallest of efforts you can make cranberries tumble instead of plain old pour, or stir, or the boring everydayness of just adding them into the pie filling, made me smile. – KS

Deconstructing articles

Here's a simple activity you can do with a well-written article in order to learn from it. Maybe you're not quite sure why you liked it so much. This exercise is an article autopsy that slows your reading down and enables you to learn from the work of other writers.

Choose an article you think is strongly written. Read it twice. With a highlighter in hand and a notebook beside you, consider these questions:

- How does the writer begin the article?

- Where is the hook—that brief, compelling section that clinches your interest?

- What is the angle of this article and what is the one line or paragraph that convinces you of that?

- What metaphors did the writer use?

- Where are the transitions from one section to another?

- Who are the experts and why do you think the writer chose them?

- Where is the descriptive language? Circle those parts.

- Does the writer go back in time? How?

- How does the writer present "boring but important" material?

- How does the writer end the piece? Does the ending hearken back to the beginning?

Try this:

Find a long article in a good magazine and perform an article autopsy—keep in mind that for these autopsies, we are discovering what makes a piece live and not what killed it. Look for an article that spans pages. Do the same thing with a shorter article that only takes up a half or one page. Why do these articles work? What would you do differently?

Where do great ideas come from?

The world is stuffed full of things to write about, like an overflowing Christmas stocking. Ideas are everywhere. And if you write well, you can write well about almost anything. Readers will be drawn into the account of your bathroom renovation because of how clearly you describe the faucets and the disastrous conversation you had with Hank, the man doing the work.

"Write what you know" is the advice given to writers, especially in the beginning. That is good advice, but it's not the only true thing. Write what you don't know, and watch the world of writing open up to you. This advice is true for journalists as well as essayists or even book authors. The trick is to know how to write. If you were a carpenter, or an artist on canvas, you would learn how to hold and wield a hammer, or how yellow and blue mix to make green. Then you could build a cabinet or a table, or paint a picture of an oak tree or the Eiffel Tower.

Just learn how to write. When you know how to write, you can write about anything. And be curious about the world, other people, and what is happening inside of yourself. Writers are curious. They follow their noses and their hearts.

We believe the skills you develop as a writer are as transferable as any skill in the world. You can write about the election in your town and how Roger Smith was robbed of his seat on council, or you can write about a national election campaign with federal parties dueling it out. You can research and write how to build a barn or bake a cake. The tools are the same. You will become better over time if you take yourself and your craft seriously—that is for sure—and the stories available to you to write about and publish will likely increase in number and significance.

In our writing careers, we have written articles about post-traumatic stress disorder in soldiers, women academic deans in seminaries, scandals in charities, theological education in North America, refugee camps in South Sudan, and a long list of lighter topics, such as how to do hospitality well and learning how to make pickles. We have written and edited books about churches reaching out into their communities, the theology within The Lord's Prayer, maternal mortality in East Africa, and the state of evangelicalism on planet Earth.

We aren't experts in those fields. We are writers.

A writer needs to know how to:

- identify a great idea

- pitch it to an editor

- find excellent sources

- do thorough and professional interviews

- write in an engaging style

- write to word count

- self-edit

- meet a deadline.

The non-fiction writer who strives to write about more than themselves and their own experiences (as important as those experiences might be) must create and then select tools from a writer's toolbox. With those tools, writers can write about almost anything and write everything from blogs to articles to books to speeches to news releases about ice cream cones covered in gold leaf, which, yes, we have written.

So where do ideas come from? They may appear before you like a rainbow and be just as sudden and dramatic. They may come to you like a small mouth bass at the end of your line after you've fished for hours and you are stiff and annoyed.

Ideas come from your daily life and from the daily newspaper.

If something is bothering you, it is likely bothering other people too. If you have a pressing concern, that concern is likely pressing on others as well. If you have a question about something, you are not alone. Ideas come from comments people make or an observation by your neighbor. Ideas come from reading and thinking. They come from being observant and engaged in the world around you.

Ask questions about the world.

Why?

Why not?

What if?

So what?

What next?

What better way?

Who else?

Where else?

When else?

How can it be fixed?

Who cares?

Welcome experience

This is advice from P.D. James in *Time to Be in Earnest*: "This means going through life with all senses open; observing, feeling, relating to other people," she explains. "Nothing that happens to a writer need ever be lost." And while you're having those experiences, pay attention.

Carry a notebook and a pen

Carry them with you always, or use the notes app on your phone to jot down a thought. In *Bird by Bird: Some Instructions on Writing and Life*, Anne Lamott writes, "There is ecstasy in paying attention." Everywhere there are things to write about. Be mindful. "The writer is a person who is standing apart, like the cheese in 'The Farmer in the Dell' standing there alone but deciding to take a few notes," says Lamott. We love that. Be the cheese.

Clip what catches your eye

Create a paper file, the old-fashioned way, and collect articles that interest you or spark ideas. Use sites like Pinterest to pin articles you like, ideas that inspire you and that you would like to write about, or articles and themes that stir something in you.

Extrapolate

You can extrapolate up or extrapolate down. Either way, this way of thinking means taking something obvious and turning it on its head, or just pulling apart the strands to see what else is going on. In *The Art and Craft of Feature Writing*, William E. Blundell suggests two questions a reporter can ask: "What is the probable principal cause of this single development?" and, will that cause create "similar effects in other places on other people and organizations?" With this technique, you interrogate the obvious to find out what else might be going on. During the first weeks of Pope Francis's papacy, we saw a piece on the small tailor shop in Rome that creates the Pope's liturgical garb. It was a fascinating read and a charming profile of a tailor and his business, and we are sure the idea came from a good writer extrapolating from the major world event of a new pope. Look for the unusual, neglected story. Go big in your thinking, and then go small and see what you find. Go for the slightly weird and you might just find a story no one else is telling.

Listen

A good writer is a good observer and intensely interested in the complications and lives of other people. Listen to your neighbors and family members. What impacts your grandmother also affects other people's lives. Maybe it's an issue for many seniors and perhaps there is an article there.

Think big and think small

Let's say you discover a church in your city that does art with street involved youth, to care for them and build their confidence. That's a great local story about one church doing a cool thing. Is it a national story? It might be. Is there a movement afoot of using art to help young people? Is there a national ministry of art for young people? Why does art help people? How does art help? Look for the strands of connection between little and big, local, national, and even global.

Think about trends, current events, and seasonal stories

Keep your eyes and ears open for trends. It's best if you don't chase them but get out ahead of them. Magazines often publish articles that highlight the latest—or the next—trend. Read magazines you wouldn't normally read; most of them are available online. Or, do the old-fashioned thing and spend an afternoon at the library with a notebook and a pile of magazines. Flip through them. Your idea for how refugee families adapt to North American Christmas celebrations needs to be pitched in the spring or summer though, not during the first week of December.

Consider how-to and lists

Magazines and some newspaper departments often feature stories that help readers learn to do something new, or articles that are based on numbered lists, like: "Five things your church needs to know about renovations." We love to read these kinds of quick, practical articles and we love to write them. The possibilities here are almost endless.

Read

Read widely and well. Read newspapers, magazines, and books, especially the publications you want to write for and the kinds of books you want to write. Writers read, and they read all the time. We can't say it enough, and we will say it again.

The whiteboard technique

Buy the largest whiteboard you can afford that will fit into your writing space. There's just something about that blank, erasable canvas. List your ideas and keep that list growing over time.

Try this:

Do some brainstorming around story ideas that capture your attention. Use a large piece of paper, or a whiteboard if you have one. Write a topic in the middle and then allow yourself to think creatively and freely around that topic. Jot down the words that come to mind. Fill your board. Is there something here you could write about? Even though we've advised you to write about what you don't know, take some time to make a list of the things that you do know, because of course you can write about them as well, and you should. List your hobbies, your work skills, and your most unusual experiences.

A Writer's Life
Ideas

Story ideas can crop up in surprising places. It was at a Christian writers' conference, of all things, where it first dawned on me that Christians were definitely swearing more these days.

I heard people swearing in the midst of keynote addresses and during panel discussions—from the stage and behind microphones. They swore shamelessly, and no one in the audience seemed to bat an eye.

If people who profess to love and care about words can use bad words so freely, I thought, *this must be a trend. A trend worth exploring!*

Returning home from that conference, I started to notice other places where Christians were swearing. I heard it at a dinner party with four couples—professing believers all—and in a seminary class, which led me to believe that some contemporary Christians consider it cool to swear.

My feature article, eventually published under the title "Foul Mouthed and Faithful," explored the fact that while Christians may be late-comers to our culture's profanity party, they were cussing like never before. I noticed a trend, and I sold the idea to a magazine who later told me they received multiple letters to the editor about this article. Perhaps it was a trend that readers had been noticing too.– PP

How to find your angle

A topic is one thing, an angle is another. The angle is a way of looking at the topic, and it usually emerges after you have done some research and begun to drill down into the topic. It's both a way of approaching a subject, and your posture in relationship to it. To make things even more confusing, allow us to say that you will likely know your angle when you find it.

Here's an example. If you had noticed, back when it first began, the emerging trend of theological seminaries to offer some of their courses online, you might have pitched that idea to a national theologically oriented magazine. The topic is online theological education. But that topic is huge, as big as all of North America. You will never finish that article.

Your editor would have asked you, "What's the angle?" or maybe just handed you your angle on a silver platter, which is sometimes nice. But if you had to come up with the angle yourself, you would have begun reading and researching and doing some good thinking about the topic. Good angles come from time spent thinking. You would have read what others were writing, and maybe you would have spoken to your friend Debra, who you know took an online course in Understanding the Book of Romans just last year.

After digging around in the topic for a while, possible angles will begin to emerge. They are pathways through the vast landscape of the topic. Angles are the Trans-Canada Highway or the Route 66 of your topic. They are a way through that big subject of online education. Suddenly you have twenty-seven articles you could possibly write, but you know the publication only wants one. Your angle might be how online education deals with spiritual formation. It might be how faculty can be trained to teach online courses in the most effective way. Your angle might be how some faculty resist online education and what the seminary is doing to convince them, besides maybe firing them.

All the while, as you craft your angle, you are thinking about your editor and what your editor is thinking about. It will come as no surprise to learn that your editor is thinking about their readers and their magazine. Your editor is not thinking about your passion for the topic and how it would be kind of them to let you write about it. Not one bit. Your editor is doing their job and asking why their readers would care about this, and if this angle will sell magazines or generate clicks or be shared 1,700 times on social media.

Your editor is thinking about their bottom line and asking the harsh but essential question all writers must learn to ask themselves: "Who cares?" When you can answer that question in a line or two, you are probably sidling up to your angle. You are close. When you and your editor have chosen your angle, you do yourself a great favor by writing it down and gluing it to your forehead or taping it to your laptop, or nailing it to your desk. Refer to it often. It is your planned and agreed-upon route. It will keep you moving in the right direction.

Try this:

Choose a big idea or topic—laughter, greed, jealousy, patience, vacation, rest, suffering—and then think of an illustration from your own life that helps explore that idea. Write that story as an opening anecdote, and then just write. See what pours out. Write to understand what you think or feel about that topic. Don't censor yourself. Just write.

A Writer's Life
Angles

I'm a news junkie. I read newspapers and magazines, and I get daily headline summaries from the *New York Times* and *The Washington Post* delivered into my inbox.

So in the fall of 2016, I found the rhetoric before the US federal election—and the maelstrom after it—completely riveting. You couldn't escape the frenzy. And on social media, people were going crazy. I had friends who erupted at the first hint of anyone with a different political opinion.

All of this was rumbling around in my brain. Christians. Politics. How politics was literally tearing relationships apart. And I began to wonder how faith and theology should inform our political thinking and engagement as citizens.

I thought the subject would be a perfect feature story for a Canadian magazine, but I knew the magazine would want a Canadian angle. So I went online, searched around a bit, and learned that one of the

country's key federal parties was due to hold their leadership election in the spring. Perfect! I knew the topic would have relevance for Canadian readers. My story ended up on the cover of the magazine.
– PP

How to query an editor

If you are trying to write for magazines, journals, or websites, you will need to be able to approach an editor in a professional and compelling way. Just the thought of approaching the editor of a publication can feel intimidating if you've never done it before. Like trying to shoot an arrow into the heart of an impenetrable fortress, it's easy to imagine your idea bouncing off the publication's ramparts or arcing ever so gracefully before splashing and sinking to the bottom of the moat.

Take heart. Every castle has a drawbridge. You just need to find it.

Composing a solid query to a publication is like knowing the password that will lower that bridge, ultimately allowing you to write for that newspaper, magazine, trade publication, or journal. And while there are no guarantees—even the best queries can bounce due to poor timing, an editor's mood, the publication having recently published something similar, or a dozen other reasons—there are steps you can take to give your query the best shot of getting through and leading to an assignment.

First, editors are busy people. In addition to all of their other responsibilities, they might receive dozens of emailed queries every day. Your query needs to stand out. Here's how to make certain that it does:

- Research the publication. Taking some time to study it, noting the kinds of stories it runs and ads it publishes, will be helpful in understanding the sorts of articles its readers care about and its editors like to publish.

- Check out the publication's website. Look for writer's guidelines. There may be instructions for how to compose and send in your query and whom to send it to. Follow them.

- In the absence of specific instructions, your query needs to be well-written, original, and compelling, with pristine spelling, punctuation, and grammar. The editor will be evaluating your writing skills based on this first, introductory email.

- In a few sentences, describe the article you would like to write and the angle you will take. Include information on which experts you plan to interview (if any).

- Because you have studied the publication, include a line or two about how you see your article idea fitting into the broad scope of the magazine. Why would the readers of this publication enjoy your article?

- Explain briefly why you are the right person to write this article, providing information about any relevant background or experiences you've had that make you uniquely suited to write it. Note any related or pertinent publication credits you might have.

- Include full contact information in the email so that the editor can pick up the phone to chat with you about your proposal, if they wish to do so. It's rare for an editor to call based on a query, but it does happen. Save them work by providing your number.

- Include a link to your website and a few links to other pieces you've had published so that the editor can evaluate your work.

- It's okay to check in if you do not hear back from the editor, but don't become a nag. Wait at least one week and then send a polite reminder. The truth is, you may never hear back if they don't like the idea. It's also possible that your email will get lost in a packed inbox, so checking in once or twice to recap your idea for the editor is perfectly fine. If your idea is good enough, the editor will be grateful you did.

Research is hard work, plus fun

We wouldn't dream of setting out on a trip without reading about the place to which we were headed, or taking tips from other people's experiences who had already been there. The same principle applies to writing. Before you sit down to write, save yourself some time and do your research.

A good place to start is what others have already written. Read all you can about your topic. Use Google Scholar, Google News, and Google Books, in addition to your regular search style. We've even used Google Maps and Google Earth to learn more about the geography of a place and the look of a neighborhood far away. Google Images can show you what a source looks like before you talk to them (which can help to give you a visual of the person you are interviewing, if you're interviewing them over the phone or online).

Don't be afraid to read other writers' writing on the same topic. You will arrive at your own unique conclusions, place, and piece eventually. Speak to librarians. You might be amazed at how they can help you with your research.

Make a list of potential sources. Who are the experts? Who are the players in this story? Try to get the major characters, of course, but it's good to include minor cast members as well. In fact, getting the minor characters might be essential to bringing out an unexpected element of the story. Try to think of the less obvious people to speak to, as well as the sources everyone else would interview. The next best expert on a story could be just waiting in the wings for you to discover.

Ask others who you should interview. Ask those you interview who else you should interview. Some of our best suggestions for sources have come from other sources. And when someone gives you a name, ask, "May I tell them you suggested I call?" Known referrals can open doors that might otherwise remain closed.

Not every interviewee has to make it into your story. Some interviews can be purely for background. Leaving someone out of your story can be hard for considerate people to do. After all, if someone has given you their time in an interview, it can be tempting to think you owe them an appearance in your article or book. You don't. The only person to whom you have a debt is your reader. We try to be courteous and let the interviewee know if they didn't make it in, before the article is published.

Begin to research immediately. You build a reputation as a dependable writer by being an available one. The sooner you begin one story, the more likely it is that you will be able to handle multiple assignments if other assignments come along. Plus, you'll be able to sleep better at night. You don't really want to say "no thanks" to an editor who wants to give you a story, or a client who wants to send more work your way. You may even be able to beat your deadline, which is always sweet—for you and for your editor.

Research until you are sick of the subject, and that means over-research by about an inch. You will know when you are ready to begin to write. How? Because you will be bursting to sit down and write. You will feel full.

If you begin to write too soon, before you have done adequate research, the writing will feel difficult, maybe even impossible. That's because you have not done enough homework. You have not learned enough about your subject to have gained insights or formed opinions worth sharing. When this happens, tell yourself it's okay. Then go and do some more research. But learn from the experience. You'll save yourself time, trouble, and angst next time.

Try this:

Be a journalist on assignment in your own life for a day. Buy a small notebook and carry it everywhere. Observe scenes and sounds wherever you go. Be alert. Pay attention. Take notes. Does the bus stink? Listen. How does the coffee shop sound? After the day is over, read your notes. Repeat this exercise regularly.

A Writer's Life
Research

When we say that research can be fun, it's never more fun than when you get to travel to see new sights, hear new sounds, and meet new people.

This kind of research also has the potential to enlarge your heart, mind, and spirit in important ways. Transplant yourself into a different country, a different culture, and you may feel vulnerable. "And when one is vulnerable," writes Mary Craig in her classic book *Blessings,* "one has the humility to learn."

I felt vulnerable driving along the deeply rutted, red dirt roads of the East Ugandan sub-county of Budondo, en route to visit a Traditional Birth Attendant (TBA) in the course of my research for a book about maternal mortality—that is, women dying in childbirth.

TBAs have been trusted members of African communities since time immemorial. They function as a sort of birth attendant or midwife, but without any actual medical training.

When I arrived at the local TBA's ramshackle home, there was a heavily pregnant woman sitting in the dust outside, awaiting the TBA's return from her garden. The woman was in labor and told me—through a translator—that she planned to deliver this, her eighth baby, on a mat in the tiny, dark, back room of this home where she had delivered her other seven children.

As we awaited the TBA's arrival, I noted the chickens scratching nearby and the even-closer cow, lazily chewing its cud in the heat of the mid-day sun. I saw the pit latrine and the mud walls of the TBA's home. There was no running water or electricity. I wrote down all of those details in my notebook; and every one of them made it into the final story.

It was on-location research of the very best, most heart-enlarging kind. – PP

How to do great interviews

If you are writing articles, the interview is your best source of research. Even book authors and essay writers can benefit from interviewing people and might have to tap into journalistic skills they did not know they had. Tapping into the expertise of others can make all your writing stronger.

Of course, most of our interviews today are conducted by phone or online. But if you can do an interview in person, that is always better. Why? Because sitting in someone's office or in a coffee shop across from them allows you to make observations that will strengthen your final piece. You can take note of the décor on their office walls, the jam-packed pen holder teetering on the edge of their desk, the framed picture of their grandchild. At the café, you can notice the color of their tie, what they order, and how they order it, the look on their face as they respond to your well-planned—and spontane-ous—questions, or the nervous tic that develops at the corner of their mouth when you ask them the tough ones.

"Writers are sensitive observers of reality," says Leyland Ryken in his essay, *Thinking Christianly About Literature.* "It is part of their craft to be such." And while Ryken wasn't speaking specifically about in-person interviews, his point applies.

Research your subject. Know who it is you will be interviewing and why. If you can't find the information you need to prepare for your interview online, ask the person to send you some background in advance of your scheduled interview, so you can review it and prepare thoughtful questions.

Research your topic. You don't need to know everything before you do your interview; in fact, sometimes it's best not to. But you need to know enough to know what questions to ask.

Craft questions ahead of time. Think about questions your readers would want to ask if they were the ones doing the interview. If your interviewee asks to see your questions ahead of time, send them. It's a courtesy that will allow them more thinking time and just might result in a better interview for you. Usually you are not tied to those questions. You can still ask what you want to ask.

Show up prepared and on time. Bring extra batteries for your recording device, extra pencils and pens for note taking. Thank your subject for taking the time to speak with you, and before you begin, confirm the amount of time they have allotted.

Begin your interview by tossing away the questions you have crafted. Not really! We are joking. But don't stick to a script. Think of the questions you've prepared as a frame around which you will construct the interview.

If the interview is going well, if you give your interviewee the courtesy of listening carefully, if you approach them in an attitude of humility rather than arrogance, and especially if the atmosphere is not confrontational, your interview will quickly turn into a conversation. This is good. This is what you want. Follow the conversation to discover rich material. Remember that when you are interviewing someone, you are the reader's proxy. You have the opportunity to sit face-to-face with an expert and ask whatever you want (and whatever your readers would want to know). Don't be afraid of silence. If you ask a question and receive a short, unsatisfactory response, just wait. Resist the urge to badger or fill in the quiet moments. Wait. Your subject will likely start to talk again and give you more details or an insight that would not have come otherwise.

So ask away. And listen well.

We'll say it again because it's important: listen carefully. Listening is at the heart of the art of interviewing. It's not about you. This is not the time to demonstrate your cleverness or vulnerabilities to the person you are interviewing, but it *is* the time to allow them to demonstrate theirs. We know: the temptation is real. Resist it. They'll see how smart you are and marvel at your brilliance when they read your published piece.

Take scrupulous notes and record your interview. It's best not to rely on only one way to capture your conversation. Notebooks get lost. Recording devices betray us. Use both. Tell your subject you are recording them. Even if you are using a laptop to take notes for a phone interview, you will develop your own type of shorthand that will serve you well. Quotes must be exactly correct, so if you don't feel you have heard something correctly, ask your source to repeat it. And observe. As you interview, jot down notes if you can about what you are observing around you. Sights, sounds, smells. Carefully used descriptive touches can set your work apart.

As you approach the end of your interview, quickly review your list of questions to make sure you have covered everything you need to cover. Ask any remaining questions. Then offer your subject an opportunity to share one final thing, a last thought. You can ask: "Is there anything else you'd like to say that I haven't asked you?" Or, "What would you really want our readers to know that we haven't already discussed?" You won't be disappointed by the answer.

Thank them. Ask for permission to send a follow-up email or call them again if, when you begin to write, you realize you need to confirm or clarify something.

Keep your word about promises made. This seems so basic, but the person you have interviewed has probably given you an hour of their day and felt very vulnerable while doing so. If you've asked them for an hour—make sure you're finished in an hour. If you've still got more questions but are out of time, ask if they can spare five more minutes. If you promise to send them their quotes for review before your article is published, send them their quotes. If you promise not to reveal something they ask you not to reveal, honor your word. If you promise to have a copy of the article sent to the subject, make sure to get your interviewee's preferred mailing address, and pass it along to your editor. No one likes a broken promise.

As soon as possible after the interview is over, review your notes. While the conversation is still fresh in your mind, flesh out your shorthand so that nothing important is lost later due to indecipherability.

Try this:

Listen to a radio program, podcast, or television interview for five minutes, with notebook and pencil in hand. Pretend you are a journalist trying to accurately capture what is being said. You will quickly realize the impossibility of keeping up by taking longhand notes.

Now think about how you might shorten some of the longer, reoccurring words by using mathematical symbols, numbers, simple strokes, or even a letter or two. (The word "you" can become "u", the word "because" simply "b". Drppng vwls = ez way 2 shrtn wrds bt still b readbl l8r.)

A Writer's Life
Disaster

So there I sat in a little cozy room at the Royal York hotel in downtown Toronto, chatting to Franklin Graham and his entourage about Eliza Doolittle.

Part of my pre-interview warm-up strategy involves small talk. With Graham, I was mostly trying to relax myself. As I set up, I explained how I would be taping the interview using an iPhone app I had learned about from a journalist, Eliza Doolittle, who had traveled with Graham to South Sudan. I had heard her speak at a conference and asked her about the app. And now I use it. "And isn't that a funny coincidence?" I asked.

It was hours later, after my interview, after dinner out, after a romp through an art gallery, and after interviewing a bunch more people—when the thought slowly bubbled up into my consciousness that the odds of the journalist having the name Eliza Doolittle were very slim.

I found her book, *The Tenth Parallel,* on my bedside, written by Eliza Griswold. This is now one of my best "worst interview moment" stories. I have others. We all do. You will too. – KS

Taking notes

There's something about the idea of taking notes that can make a writer feel a teensy bit of dread. We understand. We feel dread just writing about it.

Being in the midst of a significant interview with a list of questions you have to get through with an important somebody on a tight schedule only adds to the pressure. You're already multitasking: trying hard to listen carefully, observe well, ask thoughtful questions, and act professionally and pleasantly. Can't you just forget the notes and rely on your tape recorder to do the hard work? The short answer is "no."

Trust us: good writers learn to take good notes. First, recording your interviews means transcribing your interviews, and that takes a lot of time. Besides, as we've already observed, recording devices fail. And there's nothing worse than relying on a recorder only to get back to your desk to realize that you somehow failed to get the interview. Having to call a subject and ask for a repeat interview isn't fun. Do use a recorder, but think of it as a back-up.

Even if you find the prospect of taking notes intimidating, force yourself. With notebook in hand and a favorite pen, write down key words and phrases to capture what it is your subject is saying. If you feel, however, that your subject or source is nervous and your notebook is adding to that because it is a never-ending reminder they are being interviewed, tuck it away and listen hard. Hope for the best with your recorder, and help your person relax. Develop your own shorthand that will allow you to keep pace with the interviewee—or with the action that is happening around you—while capturing the main thoughts being communicated or the things you are seeing. Place quotation marks around exact quotations so that there's no question what was said by whom. When interviewing, or reading over your notes later, if you make some kind of brilliant connection in your mind or have some sort of unique insight that is yours and yours alone, write "mine" beside it so there will be no confusion later when you go to write your article about who said what, and therefore about whether or not you need to credit an idea to someone else.

If you find yourself falling behind on your note taking while in the midst of an interview, it's okay to ask your subject to give you a moment to catch up. Just don't ask too often. That could get annoying quickly. Be the writing professional you are by taking fast, accurate notes.

We love to take notes on our computers when conducting telephone interviews. It's not unusual to be able to type faster than you can write. But don't fall into the trap of thinking you have to capture every word being said. You can get so caught up in the process of trying to do that, that you neglect to really listen to what's being said, and so miss crucial opportunities to ask jumping off questions.

Highlight key ideas, words, and phrases as you go. And if you are recording your interview while you type, and your subject says something completely brilliant or outrageous that you know you are going to want to use in your article later (or even just to check on the wording of a quote), steal a glance at your recording device and make a note of the running time at which the moment of brilliance occurred. That will make it easier and save time when you sit down with your notes later to make your outline.

Routinely check the app store for new ways to record on your phone, or to use your smart phone as a recording device. New and better apps are being developed all the time that can help writers do their recording work well.

When you write about vulnerable people

As a writer who is probably interested in making the world a better place, you may find yourself writing about the things that make the world a difficult place. Your writing might take you into tough situations, tackling complicated subjects like prostitution, poverty, oppression, human trafficking, human rights, and reconciliation, just to name a few.

It is essential to treat your sources—those generous people who have agreed to be interviewed for your work—with dignity and respect.

This is true of every person you involve in your stories of course, but special attention is required when you are interviewing people who might have a history of being exploited, or who do not feel they have a strong voice in our society.

As a writer of faith, you do not want to become another person who has exploited the subjects and their stories. You must be certain to fully explain your assignment and where your story or book will appear. Confirm you have their full and free permission to use their words and to tell this part of their story on their behalf. Are you even welcome in the community? Make sure the people you are interviewing want their story told. They are not just a story-mine for writers to dig into.

If you are writing about poverty in a community, for example, take the time and find out the full story. What beautiful things are happening in that place as well? Tell as true and complete a story as you can as often as you can. When you write, portray the very real individuals you are writing about in the way you would wish to be portrayed, and that is truthfully and with dignity. Flesh out lives, people, and circumstances as much as you can. Avoid easy labels and simplistic conclusions. Take the hard path as a writer and think carefully about over-used words like slum or hovel, for example. Are those the words your subject uses to describe their own neighborhood and the homes they have built there?

Think about labels and blanket terms and question their use in your writing, such as "the poor" and "disabled." Call people what they want to be called, and if you don't know, ask.

If you can, have someone read your work before it is published who can point out any insensitivities you have shown or unhelpful generalizations you have furthered. A sensitivity reader can help your work. It is easy for ambitious writers to become callous to the hurts of the world and blaze in and write about a topic and leave again. That is not an option for a Christian writer. Take your time. Do it right.

A Writer's Life
Tough subjects

I have written about hard topics in hard places. I once spent an evening accompanying a street outreach worker as she visited with women who were sex workers on Toronto streets. I have written about the refugee crisis in South Sudan, after visiting refugee camps and settlements.

With every difficult topic I have written about, I realized quickly that even with all my research and preparation, I knew very little. The enormity of the problems I was witnessing humbled me, and so did the strength of the people who lived in those situations every day. As I interviewed refugees in South Sudan, and the women working on the streets in Canada's largest city, I was struck by how similar my new acquaintances were to me. We were all parents, spouses, students, workers—and also how very different our lives were because of our circumstances, histories, and opportunities.

I saw the pitfalls before me as a writer. I ran the risk of over-romanticizing people, simplifying complicated situations, depicting heroes and victims instead of nuanced humans, and pretending that I understood all that I was seeing and was in any kind of position to reach conclusions.

Each time with these kinds of stories, I chose to confess my shortcomings to the reader. I wrote in the first-person and shared my confusion and my questions with the reader. That was the only way for me to do justice to the subject and to the people I met. I am sure there are other ways to handle sensitive material like this. I just haven't found one yet that has felt right. – KS

Outline and structure: boring and life-changing

Remember the outlines you had to create in high school? Those thesis statements, the horribly boring and dry topic sentences followed by the points you planned to make, using a variety of bullet shapes and fonts?

You might have thought you were done with outlines; we are sorry to say you are just getting started. We think outlines are essential. As your research time draws to a close (and research is typically a fun time for writers, maybe the most enjoyable period of not-writing before writing, an intellectual romp you hope will never end), and you know your outline time is drawing nigh, you might experience a sense of dread akin to climbing into your car to go to the dentist.

Don't run away. It's not that bad and it will help you in the end. To wring every ounce out of the dentistry metaphor, the feeling after creating your outline will be the same sense of self-congratulation you experience when the dental hygienist marvels at your flossing finesse and pats you fondly on the shoulder, like you've made his day.

A simple outline has the power to solve complex problems. An outline can cut problems off at the pass. Creating an outline means that you have to sit down with your research and comb carefully through it. This is the magic of it.

This is the forced, self-imposed pause in the writing process that means you consolidate all your research into one place, print off your interviews, read all those notes you jotted down, and comb through every bit of research you have done in whatever form it took. If you don't already own a rainbow of highlighters, invest in a package. You will be highlighting, underlining, planting asterisks, and shooting arrows all over your pages. You will be making notes on your notes and compiling an outline—a skeletal sketch of your article.

This does take time. But not doing it wastes time.

Spending the hour or two sifting through your notes and jotting down the road map you will follow when you begin to write will save you time later and improve your writing by leaps and bounds.

It is highly likely that the natural shape of the story will arise for you out of the ocean of your research. This is a beautiful thing. The structure of your piece will introduce itself to you, like a friendly stranger approaching you at a reception. As you read and sift and remember and ponder, you will also likely find your great opening sentence or anecdote, and just as likely discover your most powerful ending. Knowing where you will begin and when you will end will make what comes next—the actual writing—feel less like jumping into a live volcano.

In *Draft No.4: On the Writing Process,* John McPhee, staff writer of *The New Yorker*, tells the story of drowning in research for a huge story and suddenly remembering his English composition teacher, Mrs. McKee. "We could write anything we wanted to, but each composition had to be accompanied by a structural outline, which she told us to do first," he writes. "It could be anything from Roman numerals I, II, III to a looping doodle with guiding arrows and stick figures." The idea, writes McPhee, "was to build some form of blueprint before working it out in sentences and paragraphs."

This is it exactly. So McPhee got busy that night organizing his notes and creating an outline. And if creating an outline is good enough for McPhee, author of thirty-two books and global master of long form journalism, it is good enough for us too.

As you work this stage, be sure to reread your assignment, the instructions sent to you (or agreed upon) by your editor. What was that angle again? Will your completed research allow you to meet it? Seeing all of your notes in front of you will remind you of what you have. And you will discover what you don't have. If there are gaps in your research, they will rise to the surface. Maybe you still have another interview to do. Carefully sifting through your notes and making even more notes gives you the opportunity to discover what is missing, before you begin to write.

Here are other benefits, if we haven't yet convinced you:

- You can organize your material into nice, neat piles (or however you order it) before you begin to write. You know where everything is and can find it quickly as you write.

- You can choose the best quotes and know exactly who said what.

- You can divide your piece into different word count groupings. If you know you have 1,500 words overall, you can create mini-word counts for each section as you build them.

- You have the chance to lovingly say "goodbye" to all the great stuff you cannot use (or at least, not for this particular story), because, of course, you have an assignment to fulfill. And you care most about the reader. You care more about the reader than anyone else. You want to give the reader a gift, so you are free to not use material as well. If it doesn't fit, don't force it.

- As you dig through your notes and research one more time, you may discover some treasures you didn't know you had: such as your opening anecdote and your ending.

- You will end your outlining session with a roadmap for writing. This is the heavy lifting part of the writing process, the front-end loading. Do this work now, and the writing later comes easier. We promise.

Outlines require discipline, the kind of pull-yourself-up-by-the-boot-straps discipline your grandmother might have mentioned to you. It is easy to convince yourself not to do it, to talk yourself out of it like you might convince yourself not to exercise or skip the broccoli.

Don't do that to yourself or your writing.

Here's the thing, though: Writing is still art. We must never feel chained to our outline, as if we were a tired old pet tied up in the back yard, able to roam and wander only so far. Not at all. We might jot down an outline only to leave it behind as we romp through the fields of great writing. But we've still accomplished the goal of reacquainting ourselves with all of our brilliant notes and research.

If we are writing a personal essay exploring loss, love, forgiveness, or just telling a great true story, we might strategically choose no outline at all, so that we don't feel tied down one little bit.

In *Still Writing: The Perils and Pleasures of a Creative Life*, Dani Shapiro advises against outlines. Here's what she says: "If we know too much about where we're going, the work will suffer along the way. It will convulse and die before our eyes. We'll end up dragging along a corpse until finally, exhausted, we just give up." Gosh. None of us want that. The point is to make a conscious, mindful decision, and then, of course, to just sit down and write.

Here is all you need to create a workable outline

- A pot of coffee or tea and a quiet room

- A highlighter or a few of different colors

- All of your research

- A pen

- Blank pieces of paper or index cards

- About an hour or three or four

- A reward. Plan to give yourself a little treat for doing this work. We know that your story structure should be reward enough, but we are human. Go buy yourself some candy or something. You've done well.

A Writer's Life
This Book in Outline

This book first existed in draft form in a Dropbox folder for a period of about three years, over which we would each, during moments of inspiration—or snatched minutes of unanticipated free time—enter the folder and add paragraphs or pages, edit, revise, and then add some more.

Finally, we sensed we were approaching completion. All that was needed, we believed, was an opportunity to have a solid chunk of time together during which we could refine and finalize the manuscript. We plotted a weekend getaway to a cottage in the woods.

We packed snacks and sweaters, our laptops and a dog, and boxes of our favorite writing books.

The first night, we read our draft aloud, deleting entire paragraphs, and cutting and pasting sentences and sections of the manuscript. We were trying to make things fit that weren't fitting. We faced a sinking realization: our book on writing was nowhere near ready. Something wasn't working. Things felt out of place, disconnected, muddled up, like a heap of autumn leaves suddenly scattered.

But it was only as we worked on *this* section, about making an outline, that we realized what that something was: we'd never made an outline for this book. And we needed one.

The next morning, we tossed our first draft in the fire. Then with black marker on a piece of brown paper affixed to the wall, we began again. – PP

Remember your reader

One last but critically important bit of advice before you write a single word, no matter what you are writing: remember your reader. Remembering the reader is the most important thing you can do as a writer.

You will turbocharge your writing career if you remember that you, the writer, are not the most important person in this process.

The star of the show is the reader. This is a secret many writers forget, and it is one of the secrets to writing success.

That is not about the "what" of your writing—it is all about the "how." We need to write in a way that makes our readers want what we are writing. You want your writing to be a gift to your reader, whatever your topic.

When you keep the reader foremost in your mind, your writing will communicate to your intended audience, because communicating to them will be your priority. Do you have great material that doesn't quite fit into the story you are writing? Because you are thinking of your reader first, it is now easier to ditch it (and by ditch it, we mean save it in a file for another time), even though it is clever and funny and heartwarming. If it's not serving the story, it's not serving the reader.

Is every word choice designed to move the reader along? Do your verbs sparkle? Are your nouns precise? Have the clichés been swept up and tossed out? Has your work been decluttered like a hoarder's cabin?

The reader is the invisible and always present partner in the process. When you recognize the reader as the most important part of the story, you do yourself, your subject, and your sources a great favor. Placing the reader and their needs first is an act of self-sacrifice from which you are the ultimate benefactor. Your writing will improve. It will flow. You will become a lean, elegant writing machine. Your editor will love you because their priority is most definitely the reader. This may seem like an obvious point, but some writers forget it. Those who remember it will write better, all the time.

Try this:

Choose a highly-accomplished writer whose work you admire. For this exercise, aim high. Think of an author who has written books and works with a publisher, or a journalist whose work appears in well-known publications. Visit their website and all their social media streams. What do you notice? What do they do well? What can you learn? What inspires you? What could you adopt or adapt into your own digital presence? If they have an email newsletter, sign up for it and follow them on social media. Learn from what they do well and from what makes you uncomfortable.

A Writer's Life
Big words like Swedenborgianism

Years ago, I shared a cab with some tourists who had heavy accents and could not make themselves understood to our driver. It was both funny and frustrating, especially when they raised their voices to try to clear things up. Speaking louder did not help.

What does this have to do with the word Swedenborgianism? Every now and then I find myself working with material written by academics. Bless their souls. Their paragraphs are often built of concrete. It's all fine and dandy when they are writing for each other. They probably all speak Swedenborgianism and autochthonous-ism. But even anti-fideism stopped me in my tracks/cab.

It would be a lovely thought to imagine a reader with the time and inclination to look up those seven syllable words, but most readers don't care that much and don't have enough time.

Authors, even the super-smart ones, need to speak the language of their readers to get that cab back to the hotel. – KS

When you are ready to write

You have done your research. You have done your thinking. You have forced yourself to sit down and read everything over again (maybe even more than once) and created the simplest but most freeing of outlines. You have completed your pre-writing procrastination activities and your reassuring writing rituals. Now you are ready to write. Now you get to create art.

The first thing you should type at the top of your gleaming white word document is not a fantastic, gripping anecdote to set your reader on fire with anticipation. If you are writing on assignment, the first thing you should write, at the top of your page, is that assignment. Remind yourself of your task. Those two or three lines defining what it is that you are supposed to be producing will keep your focus tight as you begin to write.

And in spite of what we've just advised you about the advantages to making an outline, don't make the mistake of thinking that you have to know *exactly* what you want to say or are going to say before you write it. "Writing is a process in which we discover what lives in us," reflects Henri Nouwen in his essay, "Theological Ideas in Education." "The writing itself reveals what is alive."

How to write a great opening line

First lines or paragraphs don't need to be written first. Don't get hung up on them. Sometimes the opening comes later—in fact, almost always. You can start writing in the middle and then go back. Start in the second paragraph and feel your anxiety drastically decrease.

Sometimes, if you're lucky, your great opening will reach out and grab you during an interview, or as you did all your thinking before beginning to write. But even then, don't get too attached. What we think is brilliant one moment may not actually work in the end. Often, the time you spend reviewing your notes and building your outline will provide you with your very best start. It will jump out at you in a spangly pantsuit and yell: "Start your article with me! I'm perfect for you!" And sometimes, sadly, the best opening will occur to you after your piece has been published. The buried beginning is common.

A great opening gets your readers' attention. It is the bait to reel them in. The candy in the store window. And remember, no one likes to be misled. Make sure your story delivers what your opening promises.

To help, consider these questions:

Why am I writing this story/paper/article/book?
Why am I telling the reader this?
Why do they need to know this?
What part of this story can the reader relate to?
What is the most bizarre/attention-getting/amusing/moving/alarming part of this story?

Your piece can begin by:

- telling a story

- revealing a startling fact

- quoting a source

- thrusting us into action

Ending well

When you are done, please stop. But end well by:

- telling a story that wraps things up beautifully

- using an effective, concluding quotation from one of your previously quoted sources

- going full circle back to where you began

- or sometimes, a dramatic, sudden end is best

Everything between the beginning and the ending

Because you have built an outline and because you are intimately familiar with your research, as you write your piece, your mind will be freed to make the creative leaps that make writing fun and reading an adventure.

That is the truth of doing the hard work of thinking and outlining before you begin to write. The work you have done actually frees you later to be more creative. You have built a structure from which you can now swing and climb and jump and play. That boring outline becomes beautiful writing. It is the safety net from which you jump into the creative part of your brain.

Don't be afraid of great metaphors. Don't shy away from rich, colorful descriptions (of things that pertain to the story of course). Use action verbs whenever you can (but not just for the sake of it). Avoid the passive voice. Cut flab.

And always remember, you're actually not done when you think you are done. When you think you are done, it's only time to give yourself a little bit of space and time away from your work, so that you can go back to revise and improve it when you can see it with those fresh, frank eyes.

A Writer's Life
Blessed, boring outlines

I had just finished a huge article. I experienced bliss. The topic had been unwieldy: how boards of embedded theological schools (those that live and breathe on a university campus) can best guide their schools to success. Or kind of. That was kind of the topic.

And that's the point. I could have gone off in a hundred different directions with the sheer volume of my research coupled with the wide-open field of the subject. I could have written a book. A book that no one would read.

I spent two different sessions of about five hours in total reading through all of my research with multi-colored sticky notes and highlighters. Creating an outline. Then almost an outline of my outline, just to be safe. It was a bit like torture.

Then I went to bed, trying not to think about what the next day entailed, which was writing the thing. Taming the beast. To my joy, my sub-conscious gave me a gift. I woke up at 5:00 a.m. writing in my head. I tried to ignore it. I buried my face in my pillow and willed it to stop. But if I had gone back to sleep, I would have lost that work. I got up. Made some tea. I sat down and began to write.

With very few interruptions, seven hours later, a 3,200-word bouncing baby was born. It was a smooth delivery. All because of that blessed, boring outline. – KS

Voice

You are your voice. Your voice is you. If you were sitting down to have a coffee with a friend and decided to tell your friend a story about what happened to you the previous weekend on the camping trip you took in a fit of misguided optimism, you would just tell the story. You would not fret about your voice. You probably wouldn't plan your tone or the level of authority you wished to communicate with your word choice and pace of speaking. You would just speak. You would simply tell the story.

That is the natural, uninhibited flowing place we want to reach as writers when we talk about our writer voice.

The desire to impress is a problem we have seen in ourselves and in writers along the way. It is so difficult for us all to relax. We may think we need to select the most complex words available to us, or the most obscure ideas to impress or to influence. As Christian writers, we might be mixed up by our mission and a desire to tell people beautiful things about God. That goal might actually get in the way of good writing. Thinking too much about these things—all the important things we want to accomplish with our writing—is a mistake and one way that writers mess with their voice and worry too much about it. We try too hard.

A writer who has found their voice no longer worries about it, or even thinks about it much. They are writers who have relaxed into their craft, which doesn't mean they find writing easy of course (it is never that), but there is a quiet confidence they have gained through experience, hard work, rewriting, being critiqued, and continually working to be better.

"The best all-encompassing definition I've managed to come up with is that voice is the personality of the writer as it emerges on the page," writes Jack Hart in *Story Craft: The Complete Guide to Writing Narrative Nonfiction*. Hart also concedes that the writing term "voice" can be "maddeningly elastic" and notoriously hard to pin down.

Voice may seem clear and obvious in a first-person essay, but that is not the only place voice is heard. It is always present, even in a third-person article about someone else's butterfly collection. It might just be a quieter voice, whispering in the background.

Writers worry most about their voice at the beginning of their writing lives. Our advice is to simply relax and work hard at the exact same time. You have your voice. Your voice is you. You just need to realize it, and you will.

A Writer's Life
Voice

Sometimes when you are writing, you know you are in the groove. I have had this rare and beautiful feeling a few times in my writing life, and it is a welcome respite from the agony writers typically feel.

During my Master of Fine Arts in Creative Non-fiction, I received a chapter back from my writing mentor, and in one little corner of it he wrote: "I think this is a wonderful passage; you are in full voice here."

This gave me such joy. I know this sounds bold to say, but I think he might have been right. I could see that the passage he was commenting on really did sound like me, and not like me pretending to be someone else. I was writing what I knew, honestly. I was being myself, fully. And I was writing well.

The next day, I sat around a dining room table in Toronto at a friend's sixtieth birthday party. She was in full bloom. My friend is a priest and a professor, a writer and a mother and wife. She is fully engaged in her work. She strikes me as more fully herself than I have ever seen her. She has come into her own, as they say.

It occurred to me that my friend was embodying the idea of full voice for me, just sitting there and eating her cake. – KS

The personal essay

Personal experience and writing skill engage in a warm embrace in the personal essay. They need each other and they know it. In the personal essay, the writer carefully and prayerfully opens their soul and heart to the reader, offering up some of their most ordinary, tender, and difficult experiences to the world as a gift. In those pieces we find meaning.

In the richest of personal essays, the writer reveals herself, and the reader finds himself. "The story of any one of us is in some measure the story of us all," observes Frederick Buechner in *Listening to Your Life*. And that is the power and magic of the personal essay.

In the essay you write on loneliness, I see that I am not alone. This is the gift. This connection, which helps to keep us alive and whole in a hard world, happens by telling the truth. By that we do not mean we always tell everything—the whole kitchen sink filled with dirty dishes—but what we do tell is always true and skillfully wrought with careful attention to the choice and flow and beat and rhythm of the words we wrap around our very selves, our hearts.

Writer and pastor Nadia Boltz Weber spoke at the Festival of Faith and Writing at Calvin College (a conference we commend to you) about this kind of personal writing. She advised writers to write from their scars and not their wounds. We find this profound. Writing from our scars—as ugly as that sounds in itself—means that some healing has occurred. We are not bleeding all over the page, making a mess for everyone.

It is advisable, for example, to not write about divorce the very night you screamed at your husband that you wanted one. It is better to write about how you failed as a parent a few years after you grounded your teenager for six months when it should have been six days. You need time to forgive yourself a little bit and write your way into the lesson of your experience. Also, your son may ask you not to tell that story, and honoring that request must be the most important thing.

Confess to your priest, your pastor, or your good and trusted friend. But pause a beat before you confess to the world. This is not a way of stopping truth but of slowing down truth from its sometimes reckless run. Personal truth takes time, it needs to simmer. And we want to be careful with the people we love, and the people who tried to love us and failed, and perhaps especially with the people who have never loved us at all. There are different opinions on this. Anne Lamott writes in *Bird by Bird*, "You own everything that happened to you. Tell your stories. If people wanted you to write warmly about them, they should have behaved better."

You will have to find your own way through this forest.

But this is what we know, most of the time: true stories beautifully rendered can change lives and touch hearts. Christian writers above all others must always tell the truth. That means not covering our messy lives with a sugar coating, because who besides ourselves is glorified when we do that? And we must write about others as we would want ourselves to be written about.

It is just as difficult to treat others as we ourselves would like to be treated in writing as it is in heavy traffic, but that's not an excuse not to try.

For the writer of church newsletters and feature articles, of speeches and scripts, the personal essay may terrify us. We are accustomed mostly to telling the stories of other people. To turn inward to our own lives, and then outward to the world holding our own story in our open hands, is a risk. Some people may misunderstand or not like us anymore. That is very difficult for some of us. You could write a personal essay about that very thing and help writers everywhere. That's the magic.

A Writer's Life
Vulnerability

When I began my Master of Fine Arts in Creative Non-Fiction, I had to choose a non-fiction writing project that in the end would result in a book-length manuscript. I didn't know what I was going to write about. I considered writing about refugee settlement, which my church had been involved with in the last couple of years.

Then I realized that I had the opportunity to write honestly and deeply about my own life, something I rarely take the time to do, and I thought that maybe I should just do it. It scared me, partly because I thought, "Who really cares?" and I was afraid of making a fool of myself.

I dove in anyway, and I wrote a book about my life as a minister's wife. I felt very vulnerable. Having my chapters on topics like envy, disappointment, marriage, and forgiveness edited and workshopped by my faculty mentors and fellow students in a very secular writing environment intimidated me.

What I discovered, though, was that the more honest I was, the better it was. My new friends liked hearing about a world they knew little about: the church, and they liked hearing about my failures and my moments of redemption as a minister's wife. I think my honest reflections made them question stereotypes and assumptions about Christians in general, and ministers' wives specifically.

Somehow, I acquired an agent to represent me during my MFA, and I did obtain a book deal for my project afterward. But there was never a moment during my studies and writing that I did not have to choose to be brave. Baring your soul means being bare-naked in a way, and that never stops being hard.

But when you know you are broken and being fixed, when you know that you might be wrong as often as you are right, and that you are both courageous and clown, it helps. We can risk being honest because we know redemption is real. Blessed are the vulnerable, I say. They make good writers. – KS

Rests and breaks

A change is as good as a rest, they say, and we have found this to be especially true when it comes to writing.

Too many consecutive hours spent sitting at a computer, staring at a computer screen, is not good for your physical, emotional, or spiritual health. And it is not good for your writing.

If you find yourself at a stage in a project where the writing feels like torture, put it aside for a while. Put it aside for as long as you can, or for as long as you need to. And then go and do something completely different. Pull some weeds or bake a cake. Listen to a favorite podcast. Read a book. Make a snack or go for a run. And then return to your work. You will return with fresh eyes, like having been on a mini vacation. The break will have done you good—body and soul—and you will find that the writing will be easier once again.

But even if the words are flowing and the writing is pure bliss, even if you can hardly bear to tear yourself away from your keyboard because you're having so much fun, you are on such a roll, and the sentences you are constructing are brilliant, force yourself to incorporate regular breaks into your writing schedule.

We have found that having a dog can be great insurance against getting so caught up in your work that you neglect to take time out for some fresh air and exercise. Our canine friends have a way of reminding us that there's more to life than making one word after another appear on a screen. Feeling the nudge of a wet nose under your elbow, seeing pleading eyes gaze up at you from a strategically placed head on your lap, or even hearing a whimper at your office door has a way of pulling you back up to life's surface from out of the depths of your writing. We ought to listen. In taking a well-timed break, writing problems somehow get resolved, ideas come, and inspiration and energy recharge.

All this with a short walk around the block—even on a rainy day.

A good night's sleep (or even a fitful, restless one) can also resolve issues in your writing. You will wake up with a writing dilemma resolved, a sentence rumbling through your mind, or a brilliant opening scene finally revealed. It happens, often. Keep a note pad and pen on your bedside table so that if inspiration arrives in your room in the middle of the night, you won't lose it. Because if you don't write it down, you *will* lose it. Please believe us.

It is also good to take a break from a piece of writing when you think the writing is done. Resist the temptation to send it to your editor right away. Leave your piece alone for a day or two prior to your deadline.

Then, reread it.

Now, rewrite it.

You will want to rewrite some bits after leaving it alone for a few days. This is a good thing, because you are seeing your writing afresh. And, "without the ability to see our writing afresh we cannot do the necessary work," says Dani Shapiro. What was brilliant then seems boring now. What was clever on Wednesday is too cute on Friday. What was absolutely essential in the first draft seems overdone and in need of a haircut (or at least a trim) during your reread.

Time and space apart from your work has a way of allowing you to gain objectivity and recognize where you are being too self-indulgent, too silly, obnoxious, or too bold. Duplicate words will jump out at you, passive sentences will pop, and unanswered questions will rear up and demand to be answered.

"On plenty of days the writer can write three or four pages, and on plenty of other days he concludes he must throw them away. These truths comfort the anguished," says Annie Dillard in *The Writing Life.*

Remember Dillard's words when you return to your work after a break and feel only anguish. You will have days like those. We certainly have. But seldom have we felt the need to toss an entire piece and begin again from scratch.

A Writer's Life
Night writing

The addition of these "A Writer's Life" stories to this book came late in our writing process. When we decided to add them to the manuscript in our Dropbox folder, I felt intimidated.

Karen is a faster writer than I am. Much faster. I've written in her presence and been dismayed by the experience. I'm the kind of writer who sometimes needs to get the first sentence perfect before I move on to the second sentence. (I'm the kind of writer who sometimes ignores the wise and prudent advice you're going to read in the next section about ignoring the editor at your elbow.) Sometimes I just need to write, then refine, then think, then refine some more and then—and only then—write my second sentence.

I'm the pastry chef, adding the caramelized sugar garnish to the top of the cheesecake with tweezers. Meanwhile, Karen has set the table, prepared and served the appetizers, cooked and laid out the whole, scrumptious turkey dinner before her guests, and placed her pie— lovingly made with *tumbled* cranberries no less—on the sideboard.

When we were both writing in the same room together, laptops on our respective laps, Karen was tap tapping merrily away at her keyboard, composing pages upon pages (I was sure). She was so obviously *in the zone* that she was probably entirely oblivious to the fact that I was listening to her startling productivity completely bereft, staring at my single, imperfect sentence, and feeling like a writing failure.

So I wasn't surprised one day when I checked this book's manuscript and realized she had added sixteen "A Writer's Life" stories, and I had added only six. Clearly, I had some catching up to do. But I promised myself I wouldn't be intimidated by our different styles and habits of writing; I would persevere.

I spent an evening at my computer and managed to add another three stories, getting my total up to nine against her sixteen. I still had some work to do—a lot of work, and it was with that in mind that I went to bed.

I woke up at 1:30 a.m. with more possible stories rumbling around in my brain. If I was still awake by 2:00 a.m., I told myself, I would get up and try to write.

I lasted in bed just twenty more minutes before my excitement sent me back to my computer, words flowing. An hour later found me back in bed, having added three more stories to our growing manuscript.

And the next night, at 3:00 a.m., I wrote this one. – PP

How to edit your own work

You need an editor. We all do. But you don't need one right away, sitting at your elbow nagging at you as you write your first draft. Tell that editor to be quiet and get out of the writing room.

Write your first draft understanding that is what it is, a first attempt only. You will have to edit it, or if you prefer, revise it. But to be completely blunt, what you are going to have to do is rewrite it from top to bottom, start to finish. Of course, some bits will survive, but you must believe as you hack and cut and paste and delete and create again that you are making things better.

Sol Stein in *Stein on Writing* offers this hopeful take on things: "How many times in the course of a lifetime do we wish we could re-live some conversation or event, do it differently? Revision provides that opportunity. First drafts of nonfiction can be flawed in organization, quality control, interest, and language. Lucky for us writers," writes Stein, "this is the one place in life where we get a reprieve." We love this. This is the most optimistic presentation of revision and self-editing we have ever read. Try to believe this, if you can.

If you have a deadline, make up another fake one for yourself a few days prior to the real one. Don't remind yourself you are just pretending and don't let yourself off the hook. Stick to the phony deadline and be finished the first draft of your piece before it is due. Then walk away. It usually only takes a couple of hours to be able to return and see more objectively all that you have done wrong, but a solid day is even better. Two or three days is like a dream.

Left alone, our metaphors weaken. The tight abs of our writing slacken and grow loose and jiggly. That great ending? Not so wonderful after all. The scales fall off our eyes and we can rewrite with clarity and confidence. As millions of writing gurus have forever said: writing is rewriting. A perfect first draft simply does not exist.

Before you begin this essential task, consult your original assignment or the pitch you made. Remind yourself again what it was that you were supposed to have written.

Now, read through your piece from top to bottom. Fix little things as you go along, such as grammar and word choice. We'd like to say to wait and do nothing the first read through, but that is not realistic for any of us. We don't usually walk through our entire messy house just to see how disastrous it really is before we begin to clean up. No, we are much more likely to pick up the odd socks and the empty nacho bags as we walk by them.

If you see a problem, fix it.

Read your piece out loud. How does it sound? How does it feel? What can you change? Replace commas with periods. Listen for duplicate words standing beside each other like grade three kids in a class photo wearing identical shirts. Pull one of them out of there. Listen for rhythm. Is there any? Cut out the flab of most of your adjectives and adverbs, especially those adverbs. Pick up the clichés and toss them into the garbage can.

Does your opening flow or have you buried your best beginning? It is common to have an editor return your piece with instructions to rewrite it, starting this time from the fourth paragraph. Look for the best anecdote you didn't see the first time.

Have you ended well?

Now read it again looking for places you can spice things up a bit, like that last dash of chili powder before you serve things up on the dining room table. But be careful here … it's easy to get too cute near the end.

Are your metaphors mixed? Similes stale? Did you go overboard? We all do sometimes. What can be trimmed or tightened?

Does your piece flow smoothly from start to finish? Will the reader delight in your words and be so captivated by your account of the recent wrestling match that they will forget they don't care about wrestling? Or asparagus? Or whatever it is you are writing about? It is not at all unusual for one piece to go through seven or eight or even more rewrites—ideally before your editor sees it. It's okay. It means you are becoming professional.

Try this:

Read one of your pieces out loud. Is the pacing right? Are you gasping for breath? If it's already been published, what would you change if you could? Read out loud a piece you love by another writer. Ask yourself the same questions.

A Writer's Life
Leftovers

As I write on a topic, I usually have a teetering pile of books by my side, my authority figures who remind me that I don't need to have it all figured out myself. My corner of the dining room table is messy for days as I inch my way through my work.

I'm so glad we bought a long table years ago. Back then we were mostly picturing big dinner parties with loud conversations. We do that. But it is also a lovely writing home for me when my basement office is more stifling than life-giving. Or too cold in the winter.

As I narrowed in on the ending for one piece, I remembered the advice of one of my writing mentors: when it's done, it's done. Let the piece end itself, he said, instead of legalistically trying to wring 5,000 words out of every topic. As it turned out, all I know about forgiveness fit into 3,600, so I wrapped it up.

Then I gathered up all the material I did not use from the document and electronically transported it over to my leftovers file, in a big cut and paste sweep. Likely those words will remain there forever. But knowing they are in what is more of a compost bin than a garbage can makes them easier to let go of in the first place—and you never know, they may show up somewhere else someday. Always have a leftover file. You just never know. – KS

Fact-checking

The great British* writer Dorothy Sayers once wrote that "The characteristic common to God and man is apparently … the desire and the ability to make things." Dorothy may be right. But non-fiction writing is not the place to make things *up*.

There is plenty of opportunity to be creative in your non-fiction, to use your imagination to write beautifully, but you must never make stuff up. If you want to have a long and satisfying career writing non-fiction, you must not do it. Writers fall from grace too often by plagiarizing or lying. Promise yourself that you'll never be one of them.

Commit to being a vigilant fact-checker. Trust us, there is no worse feeling than seeing a published letter to the editor, written by a disgruntled reader, taking you to task for being sloppy with the facts. It's happened to both of us. It makes you feel ashamed. It makes you want to curl up into a fetal position on your bed and hide for three days.

---

*   In the first edition of *Craft, Cost & Call,* we identified Sayers as an American writer, introducing an error we did not catch into the very first line of our chapter on fact-checking. We can amaze even ourselves with the ability to make embarrassing and easily preventable writing mistakes. We spent a night in agony, and then got back up on our feet the next morning. We comforted and encouraged each other, and that reminded us how great it is to be part of a writing team. Then, we moved on.

It makes you wish you had been more careful.

At one time, magazines and newspapers had big budgets and big staffs and fact-checkers who would do the dirty work for you. Now you have to do it yourself. We know, it's a pain. We can almost hear you groaning. And we also know—firsthand—the disappointment that comes when stumbling across a great little piece of information to include in an article, only to find out that it's not true and you can't use it after all.

But the confident feeling that accompanies knowing you are sending off a fully fact-checked article to your editor is worth it.

Of course, you will want to check and double check your facts as you gather them during the research phase. Be certain that your statistics are the most recent stats available and that every piece of information you present is verified. Take nothing for granted.

You will want to haul out your magnifying glass each time you discover some tiny tidbit of wonder to include in your research notes.

Examine that tidbit from every angle, so that you know beyond any doubt that it is true.

And when you interview your expert sources, bounce your facts off them for verification. If something doesn't sound right, they will tell you. And if, in the course of the interview, they reveal something that doesn't sound right to you, or something that seems surprising or shocking, you'll want to verify that fact. In fact, verify everything they tell you (that you plan to use in your article) that you can possibly verify.

But once you've finally completed writing and editing your article, there is one final, fact-checking step you can take. As mentioned in the "How to do great interviews" section of this book, you can call your sources and read them the quotes that they have given you, which you have used in your final piece. This is a courtesy step, but it's also a good way of ensuring that you got your facts right, and that you are fairly representing the thoughts and opinions of your sources.

Being interviewed can be a nerve-wracking experience for some people (particularly if it's their first time), and offering to read or send a source their quotes before publication can be a good way of earning their trust and increasing their willingness to grant you the interview in the first place. It's also a great way to ensure you can rely on them as a source again at some point in the future.

Try this:

Call up a friend or relative and arrange to interview them about their life. Then prepare for your interview by doing research and composing a list of questions. Take notes during your interview, then write a five-hundred word profile story about your subject's life. Once it's written, do a fact check in this way: call up your subject and work your way through your story, line by line, asking them to verify or correct every fact you present. This exercise will reveal to you the importance of fact-checking. You will see just how easy it is in the course of an interview to misunderstand what a subject is trying to communicate, or get a fact wrong.

A Writer's Life
Fact-checking smells

I once had to write a story about a weekly church ministry taking place in an unexpected location on the other side of the country. This particular church cared for low income and homeless people by making it possible for them to do their laundry at a local laundromat.

Everyone has to wash their clothes once in a while, but what is a simple domestic chore for most people isn't so simple for those without washing machines, or with limited financial resources.

So church volunteers would gather each week at the laundromat, where they would serve coffee and muffins to those who came carrying their laundry in plastic bags, baskets, and bins. Then the volunteers would hand out loonies and quarters, laundry soap, and sheets of fabric softener.

It's all great fodder for the imagination, and I wanted to capture the sights, sounds, and smells of the laundromat in order to set the scene in a compelling opening. But how to do that when I was in Toronto, and the laundromat in question was in East Vancouver?

I visited my own local laundromat with notebook and pen, took a few notes, and wrote my opening paragraph. Then, just to ensure the accuracy of what I'd written, I contacted one of the volunteers who helped to run the program. I read her my drafted lines. "Is this true?" I asked. "Is this how the laundromat smells? Is this how it sounds at that time of the day?"

Verified and fact-checked, I was able to finalize the following first sentence, inviting readers into the story.

"The low, continuous hum of large, industrial machines—swishing and spinning, tumbling and drying—has yet to really begin, but the air is thick with the warm, sweet fragrance of yesterday's soap and fabric softener." – PP

Have an early reader

Writers write to be read. One strategy we have found helpful (and encouraging, and yes, fun!) in our writing lives is to have an *early* reader.

An early reader is someone who reads your work before anyone else does. The publishing industry calls them "beta readers," but by any name, they are valuable.

You've taken such great care with your writing, edited multiple drafts, and have your work to the point where you're ready to send it off. You are excited. You can't wait to hear your editor say, "This is fantastic!" But before you press "send," as one final step, consider showing your work to an early reader.

An early reader should be someone you trust, someone who reads (or to whom you read aloud) your articles, chapters, and manuscripts before you send them off to clients, editors, and publishers, and maybe even, depending on your early reader's availability and accessibility, who reads your blog posts before you hit "publish."

By "trust" we mean two things: first, that you know they won't try to sabotage your writing, and second, that if they tell you that what you've written is terrible—you respect their opinion enough to listen to them.

The Bible backs us up on this: "Faithful are the wounds of a friend; but the kisses of an enemy are deceitful," according to Proverbs 27:6 (KJV), and we have found this ancient wisdom to be true.

True friends and trustworthy early readers will tell it like it is, even if doing so causes you some pain, because they know that a little bit of pain now will save you from greater pain later. They love you enough to risk hurting your feelings by speaking the truth while you still have a chance to make some improvements to your work.

In *Still Writing,* Dani Shapiro says "We all need outside readers." Why? Because, says Shapiro, "Each one of us benefits from a fresh set of eyes."

Shapiro relies on her husband, Michael, as her early reader, and writes that, "Most of the time, he has notes for me. These notes can range from comments about word choice, to issues with the structure, or concerns about cloudy logic. Sometimes I bristle—but I usually come around."

Shapiro is doing well to limit her emotional response to a mere "bristling."

One of us (and we're not going to tell you which one) also relies on her husband as an early reader, and has been known to walk away from an early reading session feeling something akin to despair. *I thought it was good! Why do I have to rework this closing paragraph, just because he thinks so? I can't stand this! Maybe I should just send it off anyway. Maybe my editor is smarter than my husband. Maybe my editor will like it as much as I do.* But within a few minutes of pondering her early reader's comments, she almost always recognizes that he is right, and that she really can and should do better.

Early readers are genuine friends, great at detecting trouble spots in your work so that you can correct them before it's too late. Like pointing out the spinach stuck in your teeth—they care enough to tell you the truth.

Early readers find flaws. Listen to them, but don't feel you have to take their advice on how to improve your work. Don't even ask for their advice. Fixing the problem is your job. Early readers may know enough to know when something isn't working, but trust your own instincts on how to make your own writing better.

Shapiro offers a helpful list of what you want to avoid in a potential early reader: "Envy. Indifference. Comparison. Laziness. Dishonesty. Lousy bedside manner. Secret agenda. Rudeness. Hostility. Poor boundaries. False enthusiasm. Lack of discernment. Inattentiveness. Distractibility. Did I mention envy?"

We would add our own list of what you *should* look for: honesty, tact, willingness to do battle for your best interest, and patience in waiting for you to come around to the truth when you don't like hearing it.

Try this:

Practice the discipline of non-defensiveness. Choose a piece you have written and ask a friend, peer, or colleague to read it and give you their most honest feedback. Free them up to be critical (you can still ask them to be kind, but tell them to not hold back on what does not work for them in the piece). This is a risk; your feelings will be hurt. But when they give you their comments, do not defend your work. Don't explain the part they did not understand, not even one little bit. Do pay attention to what you are feeling, and offer that fully to God. But just say "thank you" to your friend.

A Writer's Life
Max Lucado-Style

As host of a podcast connected to the magazine I work with, sometimes I have the opportunity to interview writers on their latest books. When I had the chance to speak to the extremely best-selling author Max Lucado, I jumped at it. I knew my job was to speak to Lucado about his latest book, but I also knew I was going to go off-script. How could a writer like me—a mere blip on the writing radar—not ask Max Lucado about his writing process?

I wanted to learn from this publishing giant. He did not disappoint. First of all, I found out that he finds writing as painful as the next non-best-selling writer. "I'll feel discouraged, I'll throw in the towel and cry," he said. He told me how he shapes some of his sermons into book chapters, and how many times he rewrites them. It was his last step that really caught my attention.

Max Lucado and his editors and publisher gather together in one room for the "good part of a week" and read the entire book out loud, taking turns, from start to finish. "The four of us meet and sit in my living room and read the entire manuscript out loud, we read it word-by-word. We don't move from one chapter to the next until all four of us give it the thumbs up," he said. "It is a tedious process of listening to somebody else read it... hear the manuscript... we always hear things that need to be corrected or could improve. It nearly always takes us a week, to get through it. Once we do that, then we're done." – KS

COST

"A well-known writer got collared by a university student who asked, 'Do you think I could be a writer?' 'Well,' the writer said, 'I don't know. … Do you like sentences?'"

– Annie Dillard, *The Writing Life*

A business strategy

There are writers who craft business plans. There are writers who write sweeping mission and vision and values statements.

We are not those kinds of writers.

But looking back over the past two decades of our lives, during which we have earned our livings as writers, we see that a business strategy has been there all along, as plain as the mountains on the horizon. So has a mission. So have goals. Even if we haven't ever written them down and hung them on the wall.

Our business strategy can be summed up in one word: diversify. Our goal in two: earn money. And our over-arching mission in six: serve the Kingdom by being story-tellers.

Diversifying our respective writing portfolios has really been an outcome of our goal to help support our families through our writing. When you need to earn an income, and you are attempting to do it by being a writer, you take on challenges and tackle projects you never thought you would.

Books, feature articles, opinion columns, news stories, television scripts, radio Public Service Announcements, news releases, blogs, flyers, ads, social media posts … we've written them all and more. When a prospective client has called and asked us, "Could you write me a …" we've said "Yes!" first, (even if we'd never done it before) and figured out how to do it (and do it well) later.

But there is another way in which we've diversified our writing businesses. For many years now, we've each tried to have one or more steady contract or part-time positions to supplement the fluctuating nature of our freelance income. Knowing that there will be at least one regular cheque in the mail each month can help to alleviate the uncertainty and smooth out the income hills and valleys between our freelance jobs.

These steady positions have involved teaching courses, consulting, researching and writing organizational newsletters and fundraising appeals, preparing speeches and PowerPoint presentations, producing television segments and shows, and directing the communications efforts of various non-profits. They have all involved writing. And they have all helped to connect us with new industries, organizations, and colleagues, broadening our horizons and expanding our businesses in ways that never would have happened otherwise.

They've also helped to keep groceries in the cupboards.

Of course, there are other things we've done consistently again and again over the years that, while not exactly part of a business *strategy*, have been a part of a strategic over-arching effort to serve the Kingdom by telling its stories well:

- We have been intentional about learning the craft of writing: taking courses, seeking out mentors, attending writers' conferences, reading books and listening to podcasts on the writing life and on how to write.

- When we have learned something new that made sense, we've put it into practice—whether that something new was a writing technique or a way of creating a better invoice.

- We have stuck with it. Even when we've been discouraged. Even when we've wanted to give up.

- We have prioritized having a life outside of our writing lives, which has nurtured our spirits, kept relationships healthy, and given us plenty of things to write about.

Try this:

Go online and Google "writers' conference." Explore your options near and far. Choose one that appeals to you, and make it a goal to get there. Outline the steps you will have to take to achieve your goal. Do you need to begin a special savings account and forgo your daily cappuccino in order to get there? Make a plan, then make it happen.

A Writer's Life
Writing goals

Especially when I was starting out as a writer, I made it a discipline to create solid, achievable writing goals at the beginning of each new year. I viewed these goals as expanding writing horizons and going deeper. I dug up an old goal list recently and here is what I found:

- **Buy another whiteboard**. My whiteboard is my best writing friend. I make lists of things to do, I keep track, I waste time choosing colors for different projects, and I take great satisfaction in wiping it clean every now and then.

- **Take a course.** Writing effective appeal letters and crafting excellent newsletters for clients require skills that can be easily upgraded and refreshed.

- **Organize my week better.** With more clients and projects came new demands on my time.

- **Network more with other writers.** I enjoy online discussions, but rarely find the time to devote to them. What I love most of all is a good dinner and a deep talk with a group of women writers all around my vintage and roughly in my area. We usually talk about our families first and then move on to a semi-on-purpose topic that relates to our professional writing lives. I wanted to meet with this group more often.

- **Keep my office clean**. I feel better about myself and the entire universe when my office is neat. And it's usually messy. I vowed to change!

Setting down specific goals can help to go deeper into the writing life. – KS

Writing spaces

You truly can write anywhere. In coffee shops everywhere, right at this moment, there is likely at least one writer bent over her notebook or laptop, writing.

We both started writing professionally when our children were young. Our respective offices at the time consisted of second-hand desks (shared with various family members) located in small corners of our homes, surrounded by pet paraphernalia, toys and games, and laundry hampers overflowing with clothes waiting to be folded.

We made space and we made time. You can too.

Ideally, you have a desk or a table that can be your writing space. However, many writers don't have a designated, reliable space to call their own, and they make it work. Your laptop might be your entire office, and that's okay.

For years when we'd sit down at our desks, we'd have to clear away someone else's artwork or homework before we could begin. When we had a business call to make, we'd have to either bribe or threaten or creatively occupy our little ones in the hope they'd remain contented long enough for us to get through the call without someone yelling, "Mom!" in the background.

As our businesses grew and our earnings from our writings became more and more indispensable to our families—which was always our plan—it became increasingly important to carve out defined spaces for our work. These spaces were our own, and that made it easier to work. There is some psychological benefit to having a corner of your own—some kind of office—designated for writing. You can control things a little bit more in your own space, whether there is music or silence, whether it is warm or cold, light or dark.

Today, we have each claimed a spare bedroom in our respective homes. We each have a door to our office that we can close to shut out noise, and a window we can open to let in fresh air and sunshine. We have a desk and files, shelves on which to organize and store our books, a dependable, high-speed Internet connection, and our phones of course. We have large whiteboards to keep track of ideas or progress on projects. We are fortunate to have a few framed writing awards serving as art and as inspiration, and a reminder that we can do this thing.

Our offices are not fancy, but they are ours. And they work, because they allow *us* to work and to view our work with all the seriousness that it deserves.

Having now worked for years in contexts of both family chaos and writerly calm, we can say with confidence that it is not essential to have a special room in which to write. If you have the drive and the determination to build a career as a freelance writer, you can begin—and manage for years if you have to—with much less. Some cities offer shared working spaces available to entrepreneurs. This can give you some company and also that great feeling of heading off to an office. Local libraries, and, of course, the coffee shop, can also do the trick.

Work toward having a space of your own and a predictable schedule to devote to your writing career.

A Writer's Life
Inspiration

Today, my office is an inspiring place to work in. My desk faces out into the room, so that when I pause at my laptop, I can lift my eyes and look at my bookshelves, filled with beautiful books. And on my bulletin board I have pinned motivating statements, quotes, and scripture verses. I need those reminders. I take them down and replace them with new ones from time to time—sometimes from year-to-year— when it feels like their lessons have been learned.

Currently, my bulletin board features two such treasures, pinned haphazardly amidst a thank you note, income tax instalment reminders, and a kind word penned by a former mentor. One is a quote shared by a fellow writer (attributed to Dallas Willard in the book *Soul Keeping* by John Ortberg) and printed out in 36-point font: "You must arrange your days so that you are experiencing deep contentment, joy, and confidence in your everyday life with God."

The other is a little piece of wisdom that comes from Thomas Merton in *No Man Is An Island:* "If we strive to be happy by filling all the silences of life with sound, productive by turning all life's leisure into work, and real by turning all our being into doing, we will only succeed in producing a hell on earth."

The struggle is real.—PP

Equipment

You don't require much to set up a writing office or writing business, and what you do need you can usually purchase second-hand. Obviously, a computer. A laptop is the handiest to have because it's portable and you can work anywhere. If you have some wall space to hang a whiteboard, we suggest you do that, and treat yourself to some different colored markers to use on it. Isn't it funny? That's considered a treat. Most writers we know also have a deep love of stationery stores and everything that might be found in them. It must have to do with a primal appreciation of paper. This is your chance to buy some of that stuff, guilt-free.

A small, two drawer file cabinet is handy and perfect for storing that idea file we mentioned and your own growing file of your published work. You can also print off invoices if you choose to keep track that way, and your receipts for tax time when you can begin to claim your writing as a business—income and expenses.

As soon as you can, buy the best office chair you can afford. Some writers work standing up; we are too lazy for that. But do pay attention to ergonomics and take care of your writer body, which will likely be still and stiff for long periods of time. A good chair can make all the difference. Any good office supply store will sell that, plus ways of elevating or lowering your laptop to the most beneficial level. Don't get carried away at this stage, though. A writer adept at procrastination can spend months reading books about writing and weeks setting up office space. Just do what you can and then get writing.

One of the first things you might want to write is your own website. It might be tough to think of an online site as equipment, but it is a tool of your trade. It's simple to set up a free website using one of many possible online platforms. There are shells of sites designed specifically for writers. If you're not sure how to do this, find a friend who is, or hire someone to do some of the work for you. You can even barter for services. Tell your friend who can whip up a site that you will write copy for his business brochure or for her own site.

Even if you don't think you are particularly adept at creating websites, you might be surprised at what you can do with an attractive, user-friendly template and a little trial and error. The advantage of having a site is that it makes you much more Google-able, and it is a place to gather your writing, your books, your bio, your writing prizes, and most likely a blog. You can keep it basic but also keep it professional-looking. Poke around on the websites of writers you admire and follow and be inspired. Take note of the elements they have on their sites and what they feature on their landing page. Check out their professional looking head shot. Is it time for you to invest in a great photo that shows you looking at your authorial best? Do update your photo every few years, though. When you are headlining the Festival of Faith and Writing at Calvin College, we want to be able to pick you out of the crowd.

We are enthusiastic users of online storage systems. Using a "cloud-based system" means you don't need to worry so much about backing up your files. In our experience, most writers are quite artsy and beautiful people with clever looking eyeglasses who sometimes don't worry themselves over those kinds of details—until they lose everything when their hard drive crashes. Find a system that you like and stick with it. You can share projects with your writing partners—like we did with this book and other books we have worked on together. You can create folders labeled with things like "Invoices" and make things easier for everyone at tax time.

We are also big believers in clean, empty journals, ready to be filled with ideas, research, and our own thoughts and dreams. Most bookstores have regular sales on these lovely books, so grab them when you see them at a good price.

We have types of pens we like better than others, which we hide along with our phone chargers so the thieves we live with don't make off with them. Sometimes it's helpful as well as pleasant for a writer to go back to pen and paper, even if we usually do most of our writing on screen. Writing with a pen in a blank book can slow our minds down and open up space and time for ideas and a more pondering style of writing that can lead us into great, new places. Don't shut down that part of the writing life in exchange for speed and efficiency all the time.

You can invest in a digital recorder that fits into the palm of your hand and makes recording interviews painless. Your smart phone can accommodate recording apps that also work just fine. You may discover, however, that recording interviews drains your phone's battery quickly, and it is disconcerting when you see a call coming in on your phone's screen in the middle of your interview. If you do use your phone, make sure the volume is turned off, and if you will be distracted by incoming texts and panicky phone calls from your kids, maybe get that digital recorder instead, or just turn your phone over so you can't see the screen. Speaking of phones, if you no longer have a landline and use a cell phone exclusively, watch for deals and sales on add-ons for long distance, especially across borders. Ditching your landline is understandable, but don't let that limit your ability to conduct as many interviews as far and widely as you need.

Some publications will consider you extra valuable if you have a good quality digital camera and know how to take excellent photos for possible use with the article or project you are writing. You might invest in a beginner photography course for that purpose. The reality is a "one stop shop" writer can fit the needs of a publication struggling to make ends meet. Do use your phone to take photos that will help you remember the color on the wall, the artwork on the desk, the model of car, or the funny sign outside of the building you are visiting. These details will add depth to your writing and turn an ordinary article into a great one.

Every now and then scroll through the app store to see what is new that might help you in your work. Canvass other writers and ask them what they find helpful. If you're traveling abroad with your writing, investigate translation apps if necessary. We would try not to conduct an interview that way—that's what human translators are for—but in a pinch or just to say a warm "hello" and "thank you" to a subject, these apps can help.

There are also writing software programs you can download that can help keep larger projects, such as books, organized. New ones come on the market all the time, but recently we have friends using programs like Scrivener. Ask around. If there is a university or college in your town with a journalism program, give them a call and ask what they recommend to their students.

Remember, even the most straightforward article is a story, and you are the storyteller. Gather the tools around you that you need to tell your stories well. And do save the receipts (including from the books you buy about writing). Believe your accountant or that guy in the mall who does your taxes before you believe us, but usually you can claim the expenses you are incurring as you set up your writing business.

A Writer's Life
A good chair

When I was first starting out in my writing business, money was tight, so I made do sitting at my computer desk on a kitchen chair. Today's kitchen chairs are often lovely, leather-upholstered, comfy things that you can sit in for hours. But this kitchen chair was made of wood. It was hard, very uncomfortable, and definitely not meant for a writer to work in.

I was also a runner back then, and one spring, in a fit of deciding I needed to do something "just for me" (my kids were still small, my father had recently died, and I was processing a lot), I joined a running club and began to train for a marathon. I didn't want to run a marathon, I just wanted to run. Training gave me an excuse to get out of the house by myself several times a week, and the time it took to run gave me time to think and reflect and process all that I needed to.

But when my end-of-October half-marathon was over and winter arrived, I stopped running. Cold turkey. I went back to spending more hours sitting at my computer desk on that hard kitchen chair. And it wasn't long—just a matter of weeks—before I started to feel pain. It was stabbing pain that moved around a bit, from my lower back to my hip flexors to my diaphragm. But it sent me to my doctor.

My doctor sent me to a specialist, who ordered X-rays and other tests, and in the end, it turned out that I had a condition commonly seen in people who exercise vigorously, stop abruptly, and sit in hard wooden chairs. I'm serious. That's what the doctor told me.

I recovered, and the pain went away. But only after I got myself a proper office chair. – PP

Discipline

When there's no one telling you to punch a time clock (do people still punch those things anymore?) and no boss holding you accountable for arriving at your desk on time, it takes an iron will, strict self-discipline, and the commitment to develop—and then stick to—a routine to regularly put in the hours needed to build a successful writing business.

Organize your life

Treat your writing life just like a job. A real job. View yourself as an entrepreneur who is launching and building a business. That means you prioritize your work. You don't allow other commitments or distractions to take you away from your work. Once your business is really rolling, it's okay to take an extra day—or an extra few hours—off here or there, or to take advantage of the potential flexibility at your disposal. (You'd rather work 4:00 p.m. to midnight than 9:00 a.m. to 5:00 p.m.? No problem.) But do any of those things too often, at any stage, and you'll find you don't have much of a business at all.

Building a writing business will take time. You can't assume you'll be able to start earning a full-time income on the first day you sit in your writing chair. Like anything in life, your business will benefit from strategic thinking at the outset, hard work, and plenty of time to gain experience.

So if you're at the very beginning of this process, think about why you want to have a writing business and the kinds of writing you'd like to pursue. Consider your own particular talents, background, strengths, and weaknesses. We both decided to become professional writers to earn an income, but also because of the flexibility there was to be had working from home and around the needs of our growing families. And, of course, because we love to write. Yes, writing is work. But it's also fun. And fun makes the work a lot easier.

As you reflect on the kinds of assignments you'd like to pursue, do some research to learn the going market rates for those types of jobs. You will likely find—as we did—that you will have to gradually expand your repertoire of the kinds of writing projects you can confidently tackle in order to maximize your income earning potential.

Being able to write across a variety of genres will keep your clients coming back again and again, provided that you are scrupulous about delivering excellent work on time and on budget. People like to work with friendly people they can count on. Strive to develop a reputation for being pleasant and dependable.

Organize your week

There's more to running a writing business than writing. You need time for editing your work, marketing your business (which can include writing query letters, calling clients to pitch ideas, creating and maintaining a web site, a blog, perhaps a podcast to give you an Internet presence, and generating a continual stream of related social media posts), producing invoices, chasing overdue invoices, and keeping your books in order. Use a paper or electronic calendar to plan your writing, editing, and administrative tasks, and build in rewards to keep yourself motivated. Be sure to schedule occasional lunches or coffee meetings with colleagues and friends. In the absence of having co-workers to interact with all day, having a lunch to look forward to with a friend or favorite client at the end of your week or the end of your month can help to keep you motivated and sane.

Organize your day

When your daily commute is just down the hall or down a flight of stairs, you don't have excuses, such as being snarled in traffic or getting snowed in, to prevent you from your work. In fact, you may just find that you need to give yourself excuses to take breaks throughout the day at regular enough intervals to keep you healthy. So take ten minutes out of every hour. Set a timer to remind yourself if you have to—then when that timer goes off, off you go. Think of those ten minutes as your "water cooler" time, but then get back to work.

Track your time. There are great apps and widgets that make doing so easy. One writer friend we know swears by time tracking, saying it "minimizes distractions," helps to keep him focused, and "eliminates that 'what did I do today?' feeling that often hits at 5:00 p.m." Time tracking helps him know when to wrap up for the day, thus guarding against workaholism. When he's reached his weekly target, he gives himself permission to call it quits early and play with his kids. Tracking your time on new projects or with new clients is a way of ensuring you are charging correctly for various jobs. By keeping a desired hourly wage in mind, you can tell if you are over-or-under-paid on a job—just by knowing exactly how long the job actually takes.

Allow time in each day to read excellent writing. Take a lunch break. Go for a walk. Know your own body rhythms. Is your most creative and productive time of day in the morning? Then plan to do your writing in the mornings. Leave research, editing, marketing, invoicing, or telephone interviews for afternoons.

Beat procrastination

There is something that happens to most writers, even the highly skilled, highly experienced types who have churned out multitudes of articles. We procrastinate. This piece on procrastination is actually part of a process of procrastination one of us is going through right now. This is not what we are supposed to be writing today.

Who knows why procrastination happens? But it usually begins as a sick feeling in the stomach and a desire to run away from your piles of research and your laptop. We've learned to beat writer's procrastination with imagination and reward. Here's how:

First, allow yourself one short, pre-writing procrastination activity— walking the dog, making coffee, organizing your desk.

Establish a writing ritual, some easy small thing you do every time you sit down to write. Maybe it's a piece of music you listen to, or a poem you read, or a prayer you say. Maybe it's where you sit in your home or office. Maybe it's the one Facebook check you will permit yourself at the beginning of your day. When you are in that place, or doing that thing, you are signaling to yourself that you are entering writing mode, and procrastination must end now.

Now, imagine how good it will feel to have the piece done. This anti-procrastination trick is so simple, it's embarrassing. It's all in your head. Think of how badly you feel without it done. Now think about how good you will feel when it is finished.

Like our dog companions, we respond shockingly well to treats. The treat might just be coffee with a friend, thirty minutes to read a newspaper, or even some small purchased thing. The thing doesn't have to be expensive. It might be $2 worth of sour jujubes in a crinkly white paper bag from the candy shop in town, or a paper cup of French fries drenched in gravy at the mall.

Picture it done. Reward it when it is. That's our sure-fire formula for beating writer's procrastination.

Try this:

Walk to your fridge, open it up, and describe the scene. Use metaphor and simile. Is your fridge a battlefield? Are the jars and bottles lined up like members of an orchestra, ready to play? Is the lettuce alive or slumped over, exhausted? Play with words.

A Writer's Life
Rhythm and rest

There can be stretches of time between writing assignments which are a blessing in a very good disguise.

Those gaps between projects used to make me nervous, until I began to detect a kind of rhythm to them. A rhythm I eventually welcomed as rest. When the next assignment did come, I realized I was more energized for it than I would have been had I lurched from one project to another.

The word "fallow" always struck me as a sad, empty word, until I realized the farmer's field is left empty so it can be lush and green once again. I grew to see my quiet times (including vacation) as fallow time. Here's how we can use fallow times well:

- Choose not to mope or panic. If you're doing your work with excellence when you have it, trust that more work will follow.

- Read well. Take this opportunity to read good writing. Spend time in the library reading magazines you don't subscribe to and newspapers that aren't on your doorstep. See what others are writing about.

- Clean out your office, wipe your whiteboard clean. If worry does creep in, send out a few emails and queries enthusiastically (but not so you sound like you are Crazy Writer) reminding clients that you are around and ready to work. Enjoy time off. Time on will come again quickly. – KS

Writing routines

We both just get our work done. That is our writing routine. That may sound flippant, but it is a reality of the type of writing on which we spend most of our time—and that is paid writing. When you're being paid, you get it done.

We both also do creative non-fiction writing, where we are writing to explore and create, whether it's a blog or an essay or a book. That is when a routine becomes more essential. There may not be a deadline other than our own, and there may never be a paycheque. We have taken writing courses to create a structure to our writing time. We have friends who have completed online courses to learn, yes, but also to provide motivation to write, complete with assignments and deadlines.

For this book, we did an informal survey of a group of our writer friends to find out what works for others. We can tell you that food and a hot drink (no consensus on whether it's tea or coffee) seems paramount. One writer needs to be a little bit hungry. We like to be full, and sometimes we snack while we work. Some writers swear by the power of a beautiful setting, still others find a view from the window a distraction. What works for one writer—working in the wee hours of the morning—does not work for a writer who does their best creative work in the evenings. Most writers agreed, though, that after a few hours, it's time for a break.

Some of our friends work with writing partners, although in their case they are each working on their own projects in a lovely location, and not working together on one project from dining room tables, as we typically do.

Writers set goals for the day—committing to writing five hundred words or more; for others it might be spending three hours in the chair, with a seatbelt on, said one funny friend. Many writers mentioned the important role that walking or rowing, or pondering in general, has on their work. Our friends were clear that writing is not just putting words on a page—it is all the thinking and interacting and observing that comes before that moment. Walking features large in both of our writing lives. We each solve big writing problems during little walks.

We find it telling that for all the variety in responses, the most experienced and prolific writers who responded to our question about routines had in common the belief that you must just keep writing. To them, writer's block is not a thing; they just write.

If you really can't think of anything to write about, write about that. Another very experienced writer mentioned that he prays and reads scripture first. That sounds right to us.

We wish there was one magical answer about writing routines, but the variety of responses from our friends told us two things: there is no one right way, and that through trial and error (writing and not writing) you will find your own way eventually.

Try this:

Describe the room you are sitting in, and the objects within. Play with words. Paint a picture with evocative description. Return to your piece in a day or two. Rewrite it.

Deadlines

The ability to set and then respect realistic deadlines is key to ensuring business success as a writer.

By "respect" we mean that when you agree to a deadline, you not only make it your practice to complete your writing projects by the time that deadline arrives, but you do so consistently. So consistently that you can truthfully say, "I never miss a deadline."

Your hard drive crashing is not a legitimate excuse for missing a deadline, neither is having a headache. "I just couldn't seem to get it done," is not an excuse. And "I was too busy planning my son's birthday party" is absolutely not. Try any of those excuses on a client too often and you'll discover you not only won't have any deadlines to worry about anymore, but you won't have any clients either.

Life happens to all of us. There may be that once-in-a-blue-moon circumstance that crops up once-in-a-blue-moon that gives you a *legitimate* excuse for having to miss your deadline: your house burns down and your computer with all your work files on it melts, you wind up in an accident and are stuck in hospital for three weeks, a once-in-a-generation tornado touches down in your neighborhood, consuming your house and every bit of evidence that you ever had a writing business. You get the idea.

Editors and clients are human, and the humane response to any of these situations or situations like them is only compassionate understanding. If your editor or client gives you anything less, maybe you ought to consider firing your client.

Recognize that missing your deadline—even in the wake of dire circumstances—still may leave your editor or client in a tight spot. They have their own deadlines to meet, and they were counting on you meeting yours. You owe them an apology for not sending your work in on time.

So make it your goal that nothing less than absolutely calamitous circumstances will prevent you from meeting your deadlines.

Why are deadlines so critical? Because meeting deadlines consistently is the difference between a real writer and a writer wannabe. Real writers meet deadlines.

A Writer's Life
Deadline strategy

One strategy I have found helpful in always meeting deadlines is to set *artificial* deadlines. That is, if an editor wants a story sent in by September 1, I might give myself a deadline of August 15.

Having a built in "cushion" allows time to deal with unforeseen problems that might crop up: the interview I need with that hard-to-reach but critical source gets delayed, the car breaks down on the one day I had free to head to the library to do research, I caught the flu and just couldn't get out of bed on the day I had blocked out to finally write the piece. Life happens, and it happens to all of us. But with a little bit of planning and an artificial deadline, such annoyances become minor delays rather than actual *missed* deadlines.

When I returned to school to pursue my Master of Theological Studies, I found that setting artificial deadlines was a strategy that also worked well in the academic context. My papers and assignments were never late. And boy did that feel good. – PP

Diversify

We make our livings as writers, editors, and communication professionals. We know this is unusual, and maybe especially difficult today, in an age of dwindling print markets, particularly if you are interested in writing primarily in the faith-based writing market.

It is still possible, though, because we know writers who do it. They aren't wealthy, but they are content with their work and view their life as a writer as a calling, but also a way to help provide for their families and support their local church and beyond.

Some of our friends have broken into the world of monetizing their blogs, because they are such excellent writers and have been able to build a sizable following by writing well on topics about which people care deeply. They receive revenue through clicks on ads posted on their sites. Others have written books that have been moderately successful and leveraged that good showing to secure more writing contracts. Some teach. Some offer writing workshops or retreats people pay to attend, based on their success with their books.

We do not know many successful writers who are not fiercely entrepreneurial and occasionally writing material in which they are not particularly interested. Think of an artist who paints beautiful landscapes in oil and that is her true love. Every now and then she might have to pull on a pair of splattered overalls to paint a sign or portrait of someone's pet, just to make some money.

Our strategy has been to use what we know about writing and apply it to a wide variety of different projects over the long haul. We learned how to write well, and then we discovered those same writing skills could be tweaked and modified to fit what a project required.

If you have worked hard to hone and sharpen your writing skills, you might be lulled into believing it is no big deal, and that everyone can write. Everyone cannot write. You have a highly marketable skill that is the envy of many. You need to leverage it.

We have taught ourselves, sometimes through trial and error, to write a wide range of things, from brochures to websites. Not all of this learning has to happen alone. There are countless webinars and podcasts devoted to strengthening the not-for-profit sector especially.

You can be in charge of your own continuing education and take free or very inexpensive training that will add new tools to your writer's toolbox and value to your business. We have written everything from Facebook charity campaigns to blogs, and set up Twitter campaigns for charities and seminaries. We have edited books and served as writing coaches for other writers who needed a boost. We have taught seminars at Christian writing conferences and consulted in online meetings with a small charity that needed help thinking through their fundraising techniques.

Remember our earlier advice: divorce yourself from the idea of writing what you know. Consider writing all kinds of pieces about what you don't know—simply by learning the tools of writing well.

While it is wonderful and rewarding to research, outline, and then write an article or even a book that will be published with your byline (and that you can send to your mother), it is difficult to live off articles, and yes, even books, alone. They just don't usually pay enough or sell enough copies to generate an income. Many authors of even multiple books are still writing other content to contribute to their income, or maybe waiting tables.

You can diversify what you write, but you can also diversify how you use what you write. Almost always a publication will purchase first rights to your work, which means they get to publish it first. But after that, rights normally revert back to you, the writer. You are free to resell that article to other publications or sites who may be just as interested in your work and not bothered by whether they are the first to publish it or not. Here we must confess, being both entrepreneurial but also a bit lazy sometimes, that we have not resold articles often. But it certainly sounds like a great idea. The best scenario is when a publication itself contacts you and asks to reprint your article. That has happened to us and it's an easy "yes!" and another fee you can take to the bank for your good work.

Remember, when your writing toolbox is full, you can pick it up and move into other types of writing.

Over the years, we have written (and been paid decently to write):

- news releases

- annual reports for charities

- print and electronic newsletters

- speeches

- promotional pieces for charity gift cards

- charity gift catalogues

- other people's online profiles

- social media posts for charities

- reports

- appeal letters

- brochures

- blogs

- video scripts

- radio and TV scripts

And edited:

- other people's books

- other people's columns

- other people's articles

- other people's news releases

- reports of all shapes, sizes, and subjects

As companies and charities streamline and make human resource cuts, it is often the communications people who are among the first to go. That is good news and bad news for you, the freelancer. The good news is that material still needs to be written and organizations hire excellent writers who can produce quality pieces on time and on budget. The bad news is that as communications personnel are let go, more freelancers have just been released into the world—meaning more competition for you. Use the knowledge of that competition to energize you to become an even better writer.

Marketing

How do you connect with these charities and companies so desperate for your fine work?

Simply call them up, ask for their creative department (they might laugh at you because that is long gone), and tell them what you can offer.

Offer to do something for free, especially for a charity. We have both done pro bono work over the years to build up our portfolios and to place our feet firmly in the door (and to be charitable as well, of course).

Network. Who do you know? Finding steady work as a freelance writer takes a certain amount of boldness and daring. Be willing to be rejected and to feel silly when someone says no. Then, in the words of a catchy Taylor Swift song of long ago, "shake it off," and try again.

Apply for full-time jobs you don't want. If you score an interview, pitch yourself as a freelancer they can use instead. This could be a very annoying thing to do for the employer, so use this advice sparingly. But every now and then a communication job pops up. Introduce yourself, even by email initially, as a freelancer who can help them in the short-term. We have done this, and it works.

Make some noise online. An easily navigated website with active social media feeds packed with marketing tips geared to charities will help position you as a leader in your field.

A Writer's Life
Writing coach

I've never considered myself an official writing coach. On one job I was hired to edit a novel; on another, a memoir, and on still a third, I was contracted to co-write a book. But looking back, I realize that on all three jobs, I became a writing coach.

When you've been writing for decades you pick up a lot of knowledge about the craft of writing that becomes second nature. It's easy to take this knowledge for granted, until you start to work with a less experienced writer, and you realize how much they are depending on you to use your experience—like a flashlight—to illuminate the writing way.

In each case, I came to highly regard the writers I was coaching; more than that, I developed a deep affection for them. They helped me to remember my own insecurities when I was at their stage of the writing game, how much I didn't know that I didn't know, and how proud and protective I was of my words. And while all three of these writers were older than me, in each case, I felt like a mentor to them.

There were moments of tension between us—when I would offer advice and they weren't certain my advice was the way to go. But they usually decided to trust me in the end. And in the end, they usually said they felt good about that. And so did I. – PP

What writers are paid

Writers of all types, not just the Christian ones, are paid in peanuts—almost. The per word rates paid to freelancers for some kinds of newspaper and periodical writing, for example, haven't changed in decades. That is why it is so important if you are trying to generate an income to diversify the kinds of writing you do.

Some types of writing pay more than others. Ghost-writing, for example, generally pays a higher per-word rate than writing that includes your byline. As writers who are Christian, we have wrestled through the ethics of ghost-writing, and issues surrounding payment, and they are worth considering for a moment. We have looked to biblical examples such as Aaron and Hur in Exodus 17, who held up the arms of Moses in battle, doing for him what he could not do for himself and allowing God to use their efforts for His purposes. We have considered the story of Baruch, found in the book of Jeremiah. Baruch was the friend and literary assistant of the prophet. He served Jeremiah faithfully for twenty years, took dictation from him, read his prophecy to the people and officials, and when the king destroyed the prophetic scroll, Baruch wrote another. In Jeremiah 45:5, God speaks a word to Baruch that's meant to encourage him, but which includes the warning not to "seek great things" for himself, because God will reward him.

We have felt like "pens for hire" at times, and at other times, we have trusted God to be and to provide our reward.

Although we have both published periodically in what we might call the "secular or mainstream" press, we have focused our attention as writers on the world of the church. For us, that has brought joy and given a sense of meaning and mission to our work. We have tried to tell well the stories of God's people living out their faith in North America and around the world.

Sometimes we have investigated trends or issues within the church that were not pleasant stories to tell. That kind of reporting on religion is also essential, especially when it is done by journalists who love and respect the church.

If we had experienced the same degree of success in the mainstream press, it is likely that we would have made more money. Although we both needed to create an income from our writing, we also wanted our work to have meaning and be done in the service of God. We have determined, like generations of Christians before us, that it is okay to serve God and be paid in a way that helps to feed, clothe, and house our families.

There will be times when, as a Christian writer, you choose to write for free, as a gift to your church, a ministry you believe in, or a friend whom you are helping with your writing skills. That is a tithe of your time and your skills, and we think that is beautiful.

For the rest of the time, though, you can expect to be paid by the word, and most publications have a set per word amount that you can usually find online. With Christian publishing, that rate can range from .10 a word to the most we have been paid, which was $1.50 a word. Rare, but exciting. Then you simply do the math and know what you will be paid for your 500-word or 1,500-word story. Note: these rates have not increased in all the time we have been writing, from when we were both just starting out to the present day, which helps to explain why we both started out writing articles but do less and less of that kind of writing today.

If you are writing a newsletter or an appeal letter for a charity, for example, you will likely agree on a project fee. To calculate that fee, you can multiply a per hour rate that you have determined is appropriate to your skill and experience, by the amount of time you anticipate the project will take. We have, for example, been paid $500 to $1,500 to write newsletters. Our per hour rates have ranged from $25 to $85 an hour over the years. Sometimes if we know an individual or a ministry is cash-strapped and can't afford the higher end, we scale down. You may make a different choice.

As you grow in your work and reputation, you may come up with your own list of set fees, amounts that you charge to write a newsletter or an appeal letter. In our experience, most charities will ask you for a quote without necessarily revealing their budget for the project. You don't want to set your rates prohibitively high, but nor do you want to be paid in those peanuts we mentioned earlier. This takes some time to figure out, and we have both made mistakes while costing out a project. It helps if you have a more experienced, trusted writer with whom you can consult. There are also resources online to help you. Search out what a writer is paid and see what you discover. Look for professional associations you can join for freelance writers or Christian writers. These groups can be a source of information on issues like how writers are paid.

Rates do change—and sometimes rates move in the wrong direction.

It is challenging to make a living as a freelance writer, but it is not impossible. Generating a steady stream of ongoing assignments is the key, as well as treating yourself and your writing as the business you aspire for it to become.

Try this:

There are Writers Associations and Writers Guides in both Canada and the United States that do a good job of tracking industry trends and rates of payment for different kinds of writing. The Professional Writers Association of Canada, for example, offers a good summary on their website under the headline "What to pay a writer." Check it out.

How to quote on a project

It can be both exciting and intimidating to be asked to quote on a writing project. In our experience, such quotes tend to associated with the biggest jobs—book projects, annual reports, speeches for organizational presidents, that sort of thing. That's where the excitement comes in.

The challenge is to try to estimate the amount of work and time that is going to be required for you to complete the project. In order to ensure you earn a fair and reasonable amount for your work, you need to be able to estimate your time accurately. Estimate that the job will take you far less time than it winds up taking you, and you could be seriously underpaid. Estimate that it will take you far longer, and you may quote too high, lose out on the opportunity to do the job altogether, and gain a reputation for being unaffordable.

Experience helps to make the estimation easier. You get to know your own rhythm, work patterns, and how long it takes you to do various kinds of writing-related tasks. If it's a client you've worked with in the past, you will also have a sense of how responsive they are when you have questions that need answering, or how needy or demanding they are of you in the midst of a project. You will also have a sense of whether they typically love your early submissions, or send them back with requests for multiple rewrites.

Begin by evaluating what needs to be done. As you think about all of the various tasks involved in the job—everything from telephone consultations and face-to-face meetings involving travel time to interviews, research, writing, editing, fact-checking, and rewriting—write it all down. Once you've written down every project task that you can think of, look at your list. It should help you to visualize the scope of the job ahead.

Next, estimate the amount of time each task will take. Then add up all of those individual times to get a total in either hours or days for the complete project.

Now, using your hourly or daily rate (these are numbers you determine that reflect both the effort, experience, and professional value you offer as well what you think would be a reasonable price to expect someone to pay), multiply the total time by your rate to arrive at a subtotal. Add in any project materials or additional expenses. Will the client require full color, bound photocopies of the finished document you are preparing? Include printing charges. Will they expect you to courier documents to them? Allow for courier costs. Does research require making long distance phone calls half a world away? Factor in long distance fees if you don't have those covered already in your phone plan.

Finally, it's a good idea to add a fifteen percent contingency to the subtotal to cover the unexpected. There are almost always unex-pected tasks that crop up that need to be done—particularly in the course of working on a large or long-term project.

It's also a good idea to research the competition. Are other writers being asked to quote on the same job? Know what the going rates are for the kind of project you are quoting. That way, if your prospective client questions you about your quote, you can point to industry standards.

Once you decide on the price you will quote for the job at hand, double check your math and your thinking in terms of how you arrived at the project time and parameters. This is an important step, because you need to feel confident about your quote and be prepared to explain how you arrived at your quoted fee if the client asks you.

In preparing your written quote, include a description of the job, a list all of the tasks in the project scope, due dates, your fee and what that fee excludes (mailing, shipping, printing costs for example), terms (normally payable within thirty days of delivery of the finished project, or payable in installments), and your signature. We've learned to include a line on the bottom of our job quotes that indicates that should the project scope differ significantly from the tasks outlined, additional charges may apply.

Quoting jobs is a bit of a science. If you never win any quotes, you're quoting too high. But if you win them all, you may be quoting too low.

If you find the job goes quickly and you feel at the end of the project that you've overcharged your client, you can always give them a gift by discounting your final invoice. They will be pleasantly surprised. And when it comes to the next job that they need quoted, they'll likely think of you.

A Writer's Life
Good editors

When I was first starting out as a freelance writer, I made it my unattainable goal to produce work that didn't need editing. I spent a lot of time being frustrated.

Then I read a published collection of letters by my favorite writer of all time, C.S. Lewis. The collection contained Lewis's personal correspondence, thousands of letters and notes reproduced unedited. I was shocked. The spelling was sometimes wrong, the syntax terrible, ideas unformed or inarticulately explained. I realized then that even my favorite writer's writing had needed—and benefitted greatly from—good editors.

A new day dawned. Angels sang "Hallelujah!" That frustrated feeling I had experienced seeing editors' edits on my work vanished and was replaced by gratitude for *their* work.

From then on, I recognized that excellent published writing is very much a team effort.

It was a freeing—and humbling insight—one that would release me from the perfectionistic tendencies that had threatened to zap every bit of joy from the act of writing, and one that helped me genuinely enjoy the feeling that came with placing my work into a trusted editor's hands. – PP

How to make your editor happy

Editors are people too, and they can help you on your path to becoming a successful freelance writer. But here's the thing: their job is not actually to help you. Their job—like yours—is to provide the reader with a wonderfully written, journalistically sound article. Here's what editors like:

- A go-to writer who has the toolbox to write about anything. They know how to find the experts, do the research, and craft a feature or news story that does the job.

- A writer who meets deadlines consistently. In our years of writing, we have collectively missed two deadlines. That's it. And that's two too many. Be the writer your editor can count on. And you will be the writer your editor keeps coming back to.

- A pleasant writer who accepts feedback with joy. Don't throw a tantrum over edits. Your editor is just doing their job, trying to produce the best piece possible for the reader. A nice result of their efforts is that you will probably get to shine a little bit brighter because of their edit. But what if you don't agree about how they changed this or tweaked that? You can disagree, just be pleasant about it. Show gratitude for the work your editor has done, tell them you think it's a great edit, "there's just these one or two points I'd like to discuss with you …"

A Writer's Life
Push back

As an editor, I have had writers push back on edits. I've been amazed at times how angry and defensive some writers get, and how uninhibited they are in expressing it. It's not that they can't push back, it's just that they could have better manners about it all.

As a writer I've done some pushing back myself. Recently, I had a long, brilliant, shimmering starry kind of a piece bounce back. It was gutted by the editor. The shimmer and the star dust had existed only in my mind.

All that work, gone.

My first feeling was one of dismay, followed by a need to curl up on the bed and sulk. I came close to just releasing the piece, surrendering it as is, to run as the editor's version. I entertained the idea of asking my name to be taken off it completely. Pride kicked in. I thought of all the people I had interviewed for the piece. I didn't want them to think that is how I wrote. Nor did I want the editor to think I was a baby. Or a princess.

So this is what I did:

- I read my original piece again, alongside the editor's version. I could see that some of what I thought was beauty in the original was bloated blather.

- I consciously readjusted my thinking to focus on the reader and the piece and not my charming prose lost forever.

- I emailed the editor and told him I was unhappy with the edit. I acknowledged that I had not submitted what he wanted, and I wanted to work with him to produce a piece that we both could be happy with. I requested one day, three hundred more words, and the freedom to reintroduce some transitions I thought were necessary, along with an opening that better reflected my ability as a writer. He said yes.

- I put in that time, and in the end I'm less happy than I was with my original, but more happy than I was with the edit. And my relationship with the editor was not damaged in the process.
  – KS

Invoicing

Out of all the administrative tasks involved in running a professional writing business, generating invoices is one task we truly do not mind doing.

Whether it's because preparing the invoice is the last thing to be done in any project, or because sending an invoice off to the client represents a harbinger of good things to come, there's something satisfying about tying up that final loose end before moving on to the next job.

If you've never created an invoice before, tackle learning how to do it like you would any research project. There are plenty of online articles, blogs, and even YouTube videos that can teach you how.

There are probably as many ways to create an invoice as there are people who need to create them. You can draw up your own template—providing you make it neat and professional looking—or use one of the many automatic invoice-generating software tools available, including online ones.

Every invoice ought to include the following:

- the word "Invoice"—at the top of the page

- an invoice number. This is a number you choose. For easy record keeping, you could just use the six numerals representing the date, or the four digits in the current year, followed by the number in order of invoices you've generated.

- your business name, even if that is just your own personal name

- your contact information

- the client's name

- the client's contact information

- the date of the invoice

- the amount you are to be paid, which is the total agreed upon, less any deposit or installments paid by the client

- any taxes you are required to charge

- a brief description of the project that you completed on behalf of the client

- how and when you are to be paid (payment accepted by cheque or e-transfer for example)

- the deadline for payment, usually thirty or forty-five days from the date on the invoice

Once you complete your invoice, save it as a PDF document and email it to your client. Mark the due date in your calendar to jog your memory when the date rolls around. If payment hasn't arrived by the due date, you may need to chase your client.

Neither one of us has ever had a client *not* pay. We've had clients pay late. We've had clients plead for extra time and for understanding. But in our experience, no client has tried to pull a fast one by cheating us out of earned income.

We like to give a few days grace, because it's possible, after all, for payment to take longer than anticipated to arrive. It's possible that the client is just really disorganized, really busy, or that our invoice got lost in the shuffle somehow.

So first, give your client the benefit of the doubt. But when a couple of days have passed beyond the due date, then it's entirely appropriate to give them a little nudge.

It can be awkward and uncomfortable to have to call up a client to ask them where your money is when it's late. An email with a gentle reminder is easier. And if at first you don't succeed, then feel free to pick up the phone.

A Writer's Life
Chasing the money

It is a sad reality that when you are in business for yourself, you will have to chase clients from time to time who "forget" to pay your invoices, or lose your invoices, or claim that your invoices never arrived.

It feels unfair. If you're writing on behalf of a non-profit organization or a business, it's unlikely that your clients, the people you are working for—who work for that organization or business—have to chase their bosses, or the accounting department, to get paid. You've done the work, and we all know what the Apostle Paul says about the worker deserving their wages. But chasing unpaid invoices is simply one of the harsher realities of self-employment.

Because let's face it, stuff happens. And even in organizations with entire departments devoted to accounts payable, invoices—like your car at the mall at Christmas—sometimes have a way of getting lost. It doesn't mean whoever was on the receiving end of your invoice is malicious; it means they—like you—are human.

As a person who really dislikes confrontation, though, learning to ask for what is owed to me, in a pleasant, understanding, and non-accusatory way, was something that took time and practice. Fortunately, I've had plenty of both, and I can honestly say that doing that kind of asking doesn't bother me the way that it once did.

I no longer have to screw up my courage or calm my nerves before picking up the phone or sending off an enquiring email to chase the money.

Instead, I give my clients the benefit of the doubt, and trust that somehow, something, or someone, made a mistake. A simple "Hi there! I noticed that my invoice dated such-and-such for work completed and provided two months ago is past due. Can you please tell me when I might expect payment?" is almost always enough to get results. And that kind of positive interaction with your clients keeps clients coming back. – PP

Writing partnerships

We can testify to the power of finding a writing partner. Years ago, our collaboration began by job-sharing an eighteen-month long communications contract that, to be perfectly honest, neither of us was really very excited about until we thought about doing it together. What did excite us was the opportunity to split a decent full-time salary, do some creative work together, give a Christian organization we believed in a bigger bang for their buck, and eat Chinese food together twice a month for lunch at a little restaurant across the street from the client's head office.

Over that year-and-a-half we learned that we worked well together, and that working together enabled us to take on huge, otherwise intimidating projects in an easier, more achievable way. We haven't looked back.

Here are two of the projects we have worked on together:

- Book-writing. Our co-authored book project *Shifting Stats Shaking the Church* was a marathon project of Excel spread sheets, Dropbox folders, and editing each other's work.

- A news release distribution service. Together we established and (with a third partner who has a specialty in public relations) ran a news release distribution service for faith-based non-profit organizations in Canada.

We would not have tackled either of those projects without a partner. They were too big and too complicated for either of us alone.

Our successful partnership is built on:

- Trust and transparency. We trust that we make each other's work better. We trust that we have each other's best interests at heart. We can both write just about anything, but we excel in different areas. We believe that together, we can bring a client a more excellent product, in half the time and with half the effort we might otherwise have to exert as individuals. We edit each other's work before a client ever sees it.

- Clear communication. When we have disagreements, we talk about them. We say, "I'm sorry" if we need to. We highly regard our partnership and see the value it brings to our lives and our work. It is to be protected. If one of us has an idea on which the other needs some convincing to see its brilliance, we pitch it to the other as if we were convincing a client. That way it's not personal. We are forced to make a sound business case for it.

- Financial goals. We are actually in it for the money. It's true. We both share a love of God, a love of writing, and we love our subject areas, but we want to make a living. Sharing that goal of financial well-being means that we serve the partnership. We see the benefit of working together when we can. Our partnership enables us to do larger projects in less time. And we believe we are usually doing a better job.

Who can be your writing partner?

When we first became business partners, we knew each other just enough to have confidence in each other's work. We were not good friends … yet. We had enough in common—most importantly the desire to do good work and be paid well for it—to believe we could work together to our individual benefit. We had met at writers' conferences, chatted a few times, and recognized each other's ambition and skill.

Think about the writers and editors you know

- Who is trying to make it as a freelancer like you?

- Whose writing do you admire?

- Who has spoken into your work to make it even better?

- Whose company do you enjoy enough to work face-to-face in a library located halfway between their house and your own?

- What project have you worked on recently that you know would have been easier and more profitable with a partner working alongside?

Getting started

Have a conversation with a potential partner and pitch the idea of doing a project together. Be open about potential complications. Acknowledge that a partnership does not suffocate, but done well, breathes life into a writing career.

We both pursue our individual projects with great energy. We don't do everything together. But through our partnership, we have become good friends. If we are stuck or need an encouraging word while working on our own stuff, we know who we can call.

A Writer's Life:
First fight

Karen and I have worked together on a variety of projects over a period of almost two decades, and in all that time I only remember having one real disagreement.

It happened in the midst of one of our early projects—a book we agreed to edit together. We printed off two copies of the manuscript—one for each of us—and began our work, Karen taking responsibility for some chapters while I tackled others. Then we exchanged what we'd each done for polishing purposes. I don't remember much about our process after that; I just recall feeling frustrated as I began to "polish" the chapters that Karen had already worked on, because it was abundantly clear to me that she hadn't done her job. Later, when we came together for a final review, Karen voiced *her* frustration that I hadn't adequately done mine.

It was only as we began to talk things through that we realized our problem. We had both done our jobs, of course, and we'd done them well. But we each excelled at different kinds of editing. Karen was better at the big picture, substantive stuff. I was better at the details. We couldn't initially identify each other's work, because we each saw the text differently. Like the parable of the blind men who are trying to describe the elephant, Karen had her hand on the elephant's trunk while mine was on its tail, and we couldn't see what we couldn't see.

We came through that experience with a greater appreciation for each other's gifts and strengths as well as for our own. Those insights have stayed with us and served us well as partners ever since.—PP

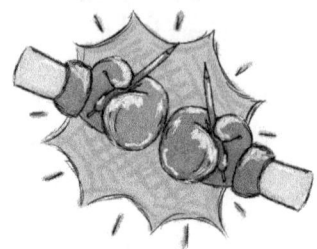

Learn

A writer's job is to observe, interpret, and explain the world well. A Christian writer's job may also touch on spiritual realities.

We say "may" touch on spiritual things because it is not a given that a Christian writer will write only about Christianity any more than it could be assumed that an American writer will write only about the United States, and so on.

In *God in the Dock,* C.S. Lewis observes, "God is not interested only in Christian writers as such. He is concerned with all kinds of writing. … The man who is weeding a field of turnips is also serving God."

But asked how he would advise someone who is interested in writing on Christian subjects to prepare themselves, Lewis responds: "I would say if a man is going to write on chemistry, he learns chemistry. The same is true of Christianity."

We couldn't agree more. So whether your interest lies in writing for the Christian market or the mainstream one, whether your particular field of turnips involves creative writing or writing about current affairs, art, science fiction, or insects—write to the best of your ability. Do it as unto God and do it for God's glory, even if you never mention God in your work.

And when you feel that you've come to the limits of your ability, expand your abilities by learning more. Learning more about your subject areas and about the genres in which you wish to write or already do write, will enlarge your abilities as a writer.

For his part, Lewis was a professor of English Literature who wrote more than thirty books, which have sold hundreds of millions of copies. Yet when it came to offering advice on the craft of writing itself, he took the position that he did not know how to advise someone how to write, because, he believed, "It is a matter of talent and interest. … Writing is like a 'lust', or like 'scratching when you itch.' Writing comes as a result of a very strong impulse, and when it does come, I for one, must get it out."

If you, like Lewis, find that you also "must get it out," one of the best things you can do to enrich both that process and the quality of what comes out is to ensure you are continually learning.

The idea of lifelong learning is so often spoken of today that it's almost become a cliché. But as long as writers write, they must also learn, otherwise they will very quickly find that they have nothing much of interest to write about that anyone will want to read. For a garden to produce a bountiful harvest year after year, the soil has to be amended regularly with rich organic matter. Continuing education is the compost that amends and improves the soil of your mind.

We have both benefitted greatly from attending writers' conferences, lectures and seminars; enrolling in classes and courses through both public and private institutions; and taking advanced degrees. Through such study we've learned a bunch, expanded our horizons, met new friends, acquired leads on possible projects and job opportunities, improved our critical thinking skills, gained new insights, tips and tricks, improved our resumes, and become better writers.

The American novelist, essayist, and short story writer Flannery O'Connor notes in *Mystery and Manners* that *any* discipline can help improve writing, including such things as (surprisingly) mathematics, logic, and theology. Any discipline pursued with passion and excellence can improve your brain's ability to think clearly, and clear thinking is important for clear writing. O'Connor believed in the benefits of drawing, in particular, saying "Anything that helps you to see, anything that makes you look. The writer should never be ashamed of staring. There is nothing that doesn't require his attention." Staring, looking closely, evaluating, absorbing, attending—these are all ways of learning about the world outside of yourself.

We can also personally attest to the richness of advanced education with one of us having pursued a Master of Theological Studies (MTS), and the other a Master of Fine Arts (MFA). We enrolled in our respective programs while working and caring for homes and families. There were sacrifices required—of time, energy, commitment, and money—along the way. But we became better thinkers, observers, and writers as a result of our studies.

Of course, continuing education does not have to be pursued in such a formal way. We've talked earlier about the benefits to be had from doing things like listening to podcasts, participating in webinars, and reading books or blogs by other writers. As both Lewis and O'Connor pointed out, ongoing learning does not have to always be focused on the craft of writing. Regularly cultivate curiosity, participate in the world beyond your computer screen, develop fresh interests, and engage in new experiences outside your door, and you will have much to draw on to enrich your writing.

A Writer's Life
Writing conference lessons

I love and I hate writing conferences. I love what I learn, but I always end up feeling some discouragement as well, usually from comparing myself with others. Now when I attend a conference I try to focus on the positives, actively network with other writers and editors, and immediately after I return home think about what I learned and want to put into practice. Here are a few enduring lessons from one conference.

- Reading during the day counts. A few speakers mentioned the good friends they have stacked on their desks to start their writing day off. And it's legal, apparently, to spend time in your working day reading well if it helps you write well.

- Do you know what else is legal? Highlighting books. This from my two accomplished roommates during the conference. It was shocking. Then liberating.

- Many wonderful published works took years and years to write. Some are warm and beautiful quilts stitched together from long ago bits of cloth.

- Writer envy is normal. Pray for those who persecute you with their success. Pray they will have more of it. You will be let out of your jail.

- Walking is part of writing. So is sleeping. You can work out big writing problems doing both of those things. And you'll feel better about just about everything. – KS

Platform

Have you ever stood on a raised platform at the front of a room and spoken to a crowd of people? Did the crowd grow because of your warm and assured voice? Did those listening to you pull in their friends and neighbors to hear you, because they thought you were so good?

Your platform is the audience and reach you have as a writer. It is your online presence, including your updated and attractive website, and it is your social media activities across a myriad of accounts and different services, with all the followers and fans you can count.

If you are trying to publish a book, you will very quickly be asked about your platform. Publishers will want to know how many people visit your website and subscribe to your blog. They will search you out on Facebook and Instagram, and wherever else you dwell online, to see your reach. If they are interested in your work and considering publishing you, they will inevitably ask you to build your platform and expand that reach. This can feel like an impossible task, especially for a writer of faith who is likely striving for humility and might already have to wrestle her ego to the ground every now and then.

There are healthy ways to view platform. It does not have to be about just being known in wider and wider circles. If you believe God has called you to be a writer, and you have worked hard to be excellent and submitted your vocation to the Holy Spirit, you can begin to think about platform as a way of serving others, and not just your own goals. If your writing is helping others, then you want them to be able to read it. How will they come upon it? That is part of your platform.

We like what Carey Nieuwhof says about this subject on his blog (and he credits entrepreneur Casey Graham): "It's a platform not a pedestal. Pedestals are about ego and adulation. Platforms are designed to be shared and used for the benefit of others."

If you write well about healthy boundaries in relationships, for example, that is an important message that others can benefit from hearing. How can you build your networks as a writer to enable that healthy, biblical message to reach as many people as possible?

If you are always putting the reader first, as we have encouraged in other parts of this book, then this is another way you can reasonably view building your platform as an act of service to your readers, present and future.

It is also entirely okay to recognize that most writers struggle with both pride and self-doubt. We want people to read our work, yet that very thought terrifies us. One moment we believe we are good enough, maybe even great, and the next we wonder why we crawl out of bed in the morning. Those feelings will appear often when trying to consciously expand our writing platforms. Be aware of them, and pray about them. Confess your unhealthy ego moments to God first, and then a friend, and confess also your debilitating self-doubt. It will help.

As you consider how you can expand your platform, here are some ideas to consider.

- Is your website up to date and attractive?

- Is it time for an up-date or renovation? Spend some time visiting the sites of writers you admire and see what they are doing. Be inspired.

- Where do you most naturally live on social media? Is Facebook your preferred online home? Do you enjoy Instagram? Is podcasting something you would consider? Where your heart is, that should be your natural digital home. If Twitter terrifies you, do not jump into those turbulent waters just yet. Observe and learn. You do not have to embrace every social network service. It is better to do a couple of things well and be comfortable with them than jump into everything and end up abandoning those streams because you feel overwhelmed.

- Consider a monthly or bi-monthly e-newsletter where you share a small piece of your own writing, but then provide other resources for your readers as well. Craft it well so people look forward to receiving and reading it. Again, do some work and see what successful writers are doing in their newsletters. Sign up for a few and read them for six months so you can understand the format, and decide what you think would work best for you and your work. Have fun with it.

- Are you a speaker as well as a writer? Ask to share at a local church group to get started as a speaker if you are comfortable.

Then build from there, exploring the possibility of offering seminars or workshops at conferences. These are all platform building activities you can share with potential publishers someday.

- Do you have a friend who can be a "platform partner?" That is a fellow writer who willingly and often shares your material online, while you shine the light on them and their work. Agree to help each other build platform.

You do not have to sell your soul to build your platform. Decide, in fact, that you are not going to do that. Move slowly, one step at a time, and don't be afraid of failure along the way. View your platform as the place from which you live out your calling to be a writer and to serve your readers, and it will be an easier thing to build.

Try this:

Start your own email newsletter. This is a solid step toward building your platform as a writer. You could include things like what you've been reading lately, links to articles you either wrote or enjoyed, a quotation you love, or some other element that connects with your writing but also serves your readers.

A Writer's Life:
Social Media

Like many people these days, I have a love/hate relationship with social media. I love it when I have exciting news to share with friends and family, or when I get to share in theirs. But I hate it when I think about how much it has contributed to my increasingly fleeting attention span, or when it sucks me in, and I find myself mindlessly scrolling past endless ads or photos of someone else's toes on a beach, rather than using that time to read a good book.

As a person who works in communications, it's impossible to consider disconnecting completely. But a few years ago, I came upon a book that caused me to think about incorporating regular technology *sabbaths* into my life and routine.

Hamlet's BlackBerry: A Practical Philosophy for Building a Good Life in the Digital Age by former *Washington Post* writer William Powers is a highly readable and entertaining book, published back in 2010 when the BlackBerry was still a thing. As an aside, it's unfortunate the publisher incorporated the word "BlackBerry" in the title and used a fun illustration of one on the front cover, because it dates the book, even though the message it holds is still relevant today. Think about that in your writing: Are you dating it with your examples and illustrations?

Powers makes a compelling case that "to lead happy, productive lives in a connected world, we need to master the art of disconnecting."

It's an art I've not yet completely conquered, but one I have been practicing enough to recognize its ancient, yet still current, wisdom and benefits.—PP

Agents

If writing a book is part of your calling and your plan, and you wish to have it published by a traditional publisher (so, not self-published), you will likely need an agent. More and more, traditional publishers do not accept queries or manuscripts directly from authors.

An agent represents your work to the publishers, sending your book proposal to them from their agency. Your agent will help you negotiate a book contract and make sure it is fair and the best possible contract for you and your project.

Having an agent who is representing your work indicates to the publisher that you are an author worth considering, or at least a writer to whom they should pay some quick attention. You have passed through the first layer of filters on the road to publication. An agent thinks you are good enough, so the publisher might indeed sit down and read through your book proposal.

You do not pay your agent until you are paid, that is how it works. You will sign a contract with your agent, agreeing that your agent (or their agency) receives a percentage of your book (normally fifteen to twenty percent), contract advance, and all royalties in the future. For that fee, your agent will likely help you refine your book proposal, maybe comment on or critique your sample chapters, and then send your proposal and sample chapters to book publishers. A well-established agent will have a list of friendly, reputable publishers who know them well, but they can send your project to any publisher that accepts manuscripts from agents.

You can Google and find many literary agents online and read about how best to approach them. Often there is a submission guideline page on their website, telling writers exactly what the agent wants to see from them. A Christian writer might want to find an agent who shares their faith, but that is certainly not necessary. Any agent can present work to any publisher, including faith-based publishing houses.

Consider the authors and books you love, and scan the acknowledgement pages of their recent works. Undoubtedly, they will thank their agent, giving you the agent's name. You can then do some investigating to see if you think the agent might be a fit, and contact them as per the instructions on their site. Finding an agent can be as difficult as finding a publisher, but once you have signed with an agent, it can make finding a publisher easier and more likely.

A Writer's Life
Writing contests

Writing awards are sweet and sour. Like my mother's famous meatballs. Only worse. The first time I entered a piece in a writing contest, I was secretly certain that I would/could/should win. That is the writer's ego rearing its head. We are all a strange combination of ego and insecurity, both of which can reign supreme at different times.

I did not win that time, or lots of other times.

But I tried again and eventually I did win some awards. It is sweet to win. Sour to lose. And generally, it can be helpful to enter.

If nothing else, entering a writing contest gives you a reason to sift through your work from the previous year and choose the work of which you are the most proud, and also just experience a retrospective of what you produced that year. This forced "year in review" of your own writing can help you think about where you want your writing to be this time next year and to come up with goals to get you there. If they are offered by the contest judges, comments can be helpful. That piece you thought was so terrific did not hit home after all, and you get to read why that might have been.

And winning? Well, that's just fun. Winning is something you can share with people who love you enough to tolerate hearing about it. Once or twice. You can throw "award-winning" in front of your name like a flashing neon sign. Winning builds confidence. It is rewarding.

I still remember the feeling of consistently coming in last at track and field events as a dorky girl. Losing is never as much fun. But it can help us too. It's not a bad thing to have your writer ego take a beating every now and then … kind of a mild, soul spanking to remind you that you can always be better at your craft. Once, a judge wrote that if good writing was orange juice, my piece was Tang. Ouch and ick. Sweet and sour. – KS

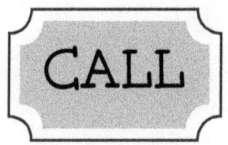

CALL

"This is the true joy in life, being used for a purpose recognized by yourself as a mighty one."

– George Bernard Shaw

A special call

As writers who are Christian, we also believe that ours—and yours—is a special calling. As British theologian and missionary Lesslie Newbigin observes in his essay, Evangelism in the Context of Secularization, "The primary action of the church in the world is the action of its members in their daily work." Your action, in your writing life, is a part of the action of the larger church in the world. That can be a humbling thought.

Writers also play a central role in the church, or they should. We are the story-tellers of the community. We write of the church, out of the church, and also to the church. We translate the church to the world, but also sometimes call the church to be better than it is already. We name things. We point and ponder. We show and tell important things and beautiful and painful true stories.

Ours is a faith centered in the One True God who self-discloses in the written Word. We are in the midst of a consumer culture—an age thick with propaganda, political agendas, corporate speak, public relations, and advertising. Truth is often taken to be relative and words begin to lose their meaning. There has never been a more critical time for the church, and her writers, to write true and to write beautifully.

Doing so will mean training, educating, and nurturing Christian writers and communicators. It will mean encouraging the stewardship of—and vigilant care for—words and their meanings. It will mean recognizing in our time and through the power of contemporary technologies that the written word can be missional. God can send forth words now like never before. And it will mean understanding that those words may hold the power to influence hearts, challenge minds, and change lives for God's glory.

It will always mean, no matter what else, telling a good story really well.

"The primal artistic act was God's creation of the universe out of chaos, shaping the formless into form," observes Laurence Perrine in *Sound and Sense,* "and every artist since, on a lesser scale, has sought to imitate him."

Imitate Him well. This is your calling.

Try this:

Everyone can be a mentor. Maybe it's your turn. Who can you help along in their writing journey? Reach out to a writer who might be in an earlier stage of their writing and take them out for coffee. Be an encourager, on purpose, to other writers. This is good for your soul, and also good for the writing community.

A Writer's Life:
Theology by heart

I have journaled off and on—but more off than on—almost my entire life. I've journaled in spiral notebooks, in foolscap-filled binders, private files on my computer, and in beautiful, leather-bound books. But the one thing almost all of my adult journal entries have held in common is that they have been letters. Letters to God.

My journaling habit began on my tenth birthday, when I received a small, yellow book as a gift. It had a picture of a daisy and the words "Private Diary" in red script on the front cover. A little metal lock on the outside ensured its secrets would stay that way. Attached to the diary—with a burgundy thread looped through its closure—was a tiny key.

I loved that diary. I poured out my ten-year-old heart onto its pages, always starting my entries with "Dear Diary," before recounting the events of my days.

But it wasn't long before addressing my thoughts and feelings to my diary left me wanting more. I longed for real communication. If I was going to spill the contents of my soul, I wanted to know that someone was actually listening. So I started addressing my entries to God. "Dear God," I would begin. I've continued that practice in my journaling ever since.

It's only recently that I've learned that theologians have a term for what I've been doing all these years. It's called "theological reflection," and according to the book *Theological Reflection: Methods* by Elaine Graham, Heather Walton, and Frances Ward, transforming "heart-felt inner experience into a theological resource," through written documents is also known as, "Theology by Heart." I recommend this practice. —PP

A Christian way of thinking about non-fiction writing

As writers who are Christian, we are writers like any other writers. To succeed, we need to be excellent at our craft, work hard, persevere, and take risks.

As we worked our way through this book, we thought about some of the essentials that don't fit so neatly into the categories of craft, or even call or cost. Perhaps they are more about character, or the non-negotiable beliefs that are the foundation for the decisions we make around our craft, calling, and the cost we are willing to pay to build a life as a writer. Here is what we think:

- Writing matters. It is a vocation worthy of pursuit, a calling to be embraced. God uses words. He uses them well. Words can deliver blessings or curses, life or death. They matter. When we write into and out of our faith, we are joining in an ancient and ongoing conversation, and that is beautiful.

- God desires truth in our inner places (Psalm 51:6). And in our writing. We write what is true. We don't lie in our writing, and pretending is lying. Plagiarizing, even a little bit, is lying, and many writers, even Christians, get caught in that horrible trap. There are all kinds of ways to lie in our writing that are not so obvious, such as changing people's quotes to better reflect what we would have liked them to say, for example, or leaving out what should be left in. We also lie when we pretend in our writing that the Christian life is simple or easy. Cherish truth and pursue it at all cost.

- We are servants of the material with which we work. We control it, but we do serve it. We need to treat our material, our sources, and our subjects with love and respect. We regard our own role in communicating our sources' words and stories with humility. We love God, and we love others with our words.

- It is a privilege to be published, not a right. Whatever we are writing, we strive to be excellent. When we make mistakes, we apologize to those we may have hurt or offended. We ask forgiveness. We learn all the time about all the things we do not know yet. We can always get better.

- We serve a generous and gracious Master. There is enough work for everyone. There is room for us all at the big table of writers, and when we pass the plate to the person sitting next to us, we all enjoy the meal more. Be generous. Be kind. Share what you know. Love other writers well.

A Writer's Life
Writers' Groups

My church for a time hosted a writers' group that grew out of an arts and faith festival held in our small town. We began the group by putting a call out on social media and through the bulletins of local churches, advertising an initial meeting of interested Christian writers who wanted to grow together in our craft. At our first gathering we brainstormed what our group might look like. We created a rhythm to our gatherings.

First, we chose a book on writing. We read it between meetings and discussed two or three chapters each time we gathered. That's how we started off our meetings. What did we like about the chapter? What did we learn? What would we bring into our own writing?

Next, we had a time to learn from each other. Each meeting someone had volunteered ahead of time to come prepared to mentor the rest of us in a skill or trick of the trade. This democracy of learning was excellent in a group made up of published professionals along with writers taking their first steps forward.

The lessons varied as widely as the personalities of the writers in the group. We had sessions on adjectives, the punishing length of our sentences, and we received writing challenges, such as a story about a young man walking his grandmother up a flight of stairs.

I'm a veteran writer. But not of fiction. As I read my feeble little story out loud (note: even though I really, really didn't want to and contemplated faking being sick so I could leave), I experienced that writers' group vulnerability where you are waiting for people to double over laughing at you, but they give a polite little round of applause instead. That's what writers' groups are for!

Finally, we ended our meeting reading bits of works in progress out loud. To each other. In the room. Out loud. Tough for everybody. Good for everybody.

If the reader wished, we offered nurturing feedback. And that was it. We were in and out in two hours, sometimes less. We alternated nights: Tuesday one month, Wednesday the next, in order to catch as many people as we could. We created a Facebook group where we posted interesting writing articles or blogs we wished to share. And that was it. Simple and effective.—KS

Spiritual care as a writer

Looking back on decades of working as writers, we can truthfully say that we have written from mountain tops and from valleys, on days when we were bubbling over with creativity and good things to say, and on days when we were not. There were days when every word was torture.

We have written from the place of feeling intimately connected with God and from the place of feeling like God was very far away. We have read something we once wrote, long afterward, and shaken our heads in wonder because it seemed as though the Holy Spirit must have been the "wind beneath our writers' wings" on that day.

Ups and downs, good days and difficult days are not just a part of the writing life—they are part of the human experience. There will be challenging times in your writing career and there is no way to ensure that you will only ever have sweet and fulfilling moments at your computer keyboard when the words just seem to pour out of you.

We believe that the mouth speaks from the overflow of the heart. So out of this same overflow, writers write. And that means that if we want the overflow of our hearts to be full of truth and goodness and beauty, then we need to take steps to ensure that our hearts contain such things.

In this age of non-stop social media, endless streaming services, and twenty-four hour news cycles, we simply must find ways to guard our hearts and to not only protect our spirits, but to nurture them as well.

How? Here are some ideas:

- Read beautiful things. Whether it's poetry or short stories or classic novels, read something every day—beyond the headlines and your social media feeds—that will feed your writer's soul. Yes, it's good and important to read to challenge your ideas, grow your vocabulary, learn, or be entertained. But it's more important to cultivate your relationship with Jesus, because that relationship will shape everything about you, including what your write.

- Spend regular time in nature. Go for a walk or a run through the woods. Sit on a hill or a park bench. Watch the birds or the waves or gaze at the stars. Doing such things will remind you of the Creator who made them, and of His great love because He made them for you to enjoy.

- Resolve now to always create your best work, whether or not someone else wants to publish it. Publication is nice, but it won't fulfill you. There is satisfaction to be felt in seeing your published byline after days, weeks, months, or yes, even years of hard work on a project. But the satisfaction is short-lived, and besides, not every writing job comes with a byline. Being "a pen for hire" without your name attached to the finished product, or even just "a pen" for your own blog, is satisfying when you write in an attitude of wanting to do your best because that is what will honor God.

- When envy, ego, insecurity, or disappointment well-up within you, recognize them for the very human reactions they are to whatever you are going through, and then let them go. In the tradition of decluttering expert Marie Kondo, thank those feelings—for alerting you to whatever underlying problem in your spirit caused them to rear their ugly heads—and then bid them "farewell." Are you feeling envy toward another writer for their blog post that went viral? Perhaps that feeling is an indication that you've been letting your own blog lie fallow for too long. Is your ego feeling wounded because you lost a bid on a great project? Turn the loss into a learning opportunity by asking your client if they would be willing to share why they decided to hire someone else. Did a critical letter to the editor about one of your articles devastate you? Pick yourself up and learn from it. Is there truth in the criticism that can help you to become a better writer?

"The finest thing we can do in life is to grow a soul and then use it in the service of humankind," writes author Mary Pipher in *Writing to Change the World*.

For Christian writers, growing a soul is not only the finest thing, it is the *primary* thing, one that will allow them to become useful in the hands of their King.

Try this:

Try to articulate your own writing goals or mission into a beautifully written prayer. Take your time with this. It is an offering as well as a writing exercise. Write your prayer and then leave it for a day. Return to it and edit and tweak, making sure you are saying what you want to say in the best way possible. Keep at it until it expresses what you want to say as well as you can.

A Writer's Life
Getting help

I had it plak'd (you know, that relatively inexpensive framing process you can get done at the photo counter at Costco where they laminate a piece of paper onto a board) because it is *the* one, single piece of published writing I have done above all others that reminds me, on my darkest of days, that I am called to write.

It is an opinion column, one that appeared in *The Globe and Mail,* a national Canadian newspaper, right at the very top of the News/Comment page.

I woke up that morning not knowing I was going to write it. I don't remember exactly what I did after I woke up, but I probably: showered and dressed; made and then ate breakfast with my family; had my second cup of coffee; threw in a load of laundry; and swept the kitchen floor—because that was my morning routine before I sat down to work in those days. Maybe I went outside to water the garden and pick some beans for dinner. Then I probably read the newspaper and scrolled my social media feeds.

But one of the stories I read—either in the paper or online—*fired* my imagination. It was about a young man—co-host of a TV show—who in a crazy competition to determine who could upset the most people, commissioned a plane to fly over Canada's largest city trailing the message, "Jesus Sucks!" All in a quest to create entertaining television. The stunt struck me as totally ironic because he was attempting to offend people who believe that Jesus taught His followers to "turn the other cheek," and that Jesus Himself did just that.

At 9:00 a.m. I sat down at my computer to write. I recall thinking, *There's no way I can get this done by noon!* And I knew that if I wanted to submit it to the paper for consideration by their Op/Ed editors for publication the following day, it had to be done by then. I remember praying, "God, help!"

And you know what? Shortly after 10:00 a.m., my opinion piece was done.

I emailed the Comment editor at *The Globe and Mail* and queried him on the piece I'd written. He asked me to send it in. I did. And he accepted it. I wasn't surprised.

I wasn't surprised because I *knew* as I was writing that piece about Christian forgiveness and Jesus' own forgiveness voiced from the cross (which was published under the headline, "An assault on Christian sensibilities, ultimately, backfires") that it was worthy of publication. And I sensed that it was the Holy Spirit prodding me, inspiring me to write. I remember praying as I typed at my computer that the Spirit would flow through me like I was a pen in the hand of God. Does that sound crazy? Believe me, when I write the words here, it sounds crazy even to me. But I prayed it. And I felt it. And I remember how it felt. In fact, I'll never forget it. – PP

Try this:

Spend one week intentionally reading op/ed (opinion/editorial) pieces. Read one a day at least. Now choose a current news event or topic that moves you in some way. Write an op/ed. Submit it to a publication, after reading and following exactly the submission guidelines on the publication's website.

How to grow as a writer

Writers are so fortunate to have the opportunity to almost continually grow in craft and skill. Simply reading an excellent book full of beautiful writing can pour into our writing lives. You will grow as a writer if you read elegant, skillful, and masterful writing often.

But there are so many other opportunities to expand your skill as a writer.

There are many excellent writers' conferences from coast-to-coast, every year. Talk to other writers about the conferences they found most helpful to help you choose which one to consider attending.

At a typical writers' conference, you will usually have the opportunity to attend workshops and seminars on different writing topics, as well as listen to a keynote address or two from a current star in the writing world. These are wonderful opportunities and refreshing to most writers. Because of the peculiar writer's soul, so easily encouraged and equally easily crushed, you may find yourself in awe of the success of others one moment, and jealous and overwhelmed by their success the next. It is okay. Share those feelings with God and a good friend and move along.

Often there are acquisition editors from publishing houses who attend some of the larger writing conferences. They are there to share their expertise, to give back, but also to scout out new talent and desirable projects. If you have the opportunity to network at a writing conference with an editor, grab it. Even if you don't have a particular project to pitch yet, try to have a one-on-one, or even a casual conversation in the coffee line with the visiting editors. They are much more likely to pay attention to the email you send them months down the road if you can say, "I met you at the writing conference …"

There are also a myriad of online writing courses, or even in person community college courses, on specialities like travel writing, for example. You might even consider enrolling in a master's program with a specialty in writing. Some of these programs are low residency and they are geared toward completing a lengthy manuscript—a great way to get a book written. Your writing will grow as professors and mentors push you and critique you at a much higher level than your average editor has time to give you in your normal writing work.

If writers' conferences and classes are out of reach for you, consider joining a writers' group, or form one of your own if there aren't any available in your community. Writers' groups vary of course, but they usually involve meeting, perhaps monthly, with other writers serious enough about their craft that they want the encouragement of other writers and the opportunity to engage in mutual discipline. That discipline might be reading a writing book together and arriving at a meeting prepared to discuss the latest chapter. It might be coming prepared with a writing piece that you will be brave enough to read aloud and then receive feedback and critique.

A quick online search will offer you guidelines to help grow writers' groups and good workshopping techniques. For beginning writers, a writers' group can help with confidence. Reading your work out loud and hearing a positive response can make a new writer feel like a real writer in a powerful way. For more experienced veteran writers, meeting with and workshopping your work with a group of peers can feel like an intensive editing laboratory. These high-calibre writers will tell you what they truly think, and often offer invaluable structural suggestions to make your work better.

In our years as writers, we have both witnessed good writers who could have been great writers give up too soon. Their skin was too thin. They did not respond well to critique, and they took suggestions for improvement far too personally. That is a shame.

Continuing your education as a writer—honing your craft—inevitably means that you know you have not yet arrived as a writer. And who ever does? We can all improve our craft and learn new skills. The first foundational skill, though, is to learn how to learn. A successful writer is a writer who can be critiqued and edited and view every learning opportunity as a chance to become an even better writer. Writers who are in it for the long-haul build writing careers, and never stop learning.

Try this:

Volunteer to write your church's newsletter, or a communications piece for a small charity. Doing so will give you experience you can build on and will be a gift to others.

With this exercise, you have reached the final "Try this" of the book, but please find us on Facebook at CraftCostCall or visit

CraftCostCall.com for more writing exercises, resources, and conversation about building a life as a Christian writer. We would love to interact with you there.

A Writer's Life
Writers to watch

Years ago, I crept away from my first ever writing conference like Eeyore on a bad day. Other people had wheelbarrows full of books and knapsacks full of trophies, or so it seemed. I had nothing. It all felt impossible. Instead of shouting "YES!" and slapping a high five on the woman sitting next to me who had just published her sixth trilogy, or even just her sixth paragraph, I felt mopey and miserable.

The fact that it was a Christian writing conference, made me feel like a layered loser: I was jealous (Bad). I knew I shouldn't be jealous (Even worse). It was a sulk-shame cycle.

It took me a few weeks to stop being so pathetic. Then I got on my knees and puffed the remaining spark of my ambition—which I had doused to within an inch of its life—back into a little flame and decided to stop being such a big baby.

It's hard to be a writer starting out. Especially, I think, when you come with a fragile wish and then are told, in that writing-conference-kind-of-way: "You can do it!" (Exciting) and then: "It might take you decades to do it!" (Not so Exciting). Or even worse: "Sweetie, maybe this isn't your thing" (Devastating).

I was reminded of my "Big Baby Goes to a Writers Conference" episode once again as I taught a class or two at that same conference years later. In the Non-Fiction basic class, I told the story of how badly I had felt after my first conference. It's an embarrassment to share, of course. I saw puzzlement on a few faces, but also a few eyes welled up and a couple of people nodded.

And you never know, they just might be the writers to watch. – KS

Publication

The first time you see your name in print, or in an online publication, it is a sweet, warm feeling. You worked hard. You came up with a viable idea. You did your research, or dug deep into your own soul and experience, and created a piece that is now being read. It is a good feeling. It can also be a frightening feeling, especially if not everyone agrees with your piece, and you experience some push-back.

There is a vulnerability to being published—to having your thoughts and your work out there in the universe, forever. It can be a bigger feeling than one might expect. A surge of panic is understandable.

People may not like you. They may not like what you write and how you write it. They might even write you to tell you that. If you are writing within the world of church publications, you might be disappointed to discover that people can be mean and nasty there too. Writing is a risk. It's okay. Be brave. You are not alone. Your heart will probably be broken a few times, and then, because you are a writer, you will probably write about that too. That is what we do.

But there is also deep satisfaction.

Holding a published book in your hands, which you wrote, can be a heady feeling. It is easy, and understandable, to believe that "if only" you can be published, especially with a book, then you will be happy and fulfilled. However, publication does not fulfill you for very long.

That is the fascinating truth that every writer—or any practitioner of any craft—who has reached a milestone moment will share: success does not fulfill the always hungry heart. We always crave more. We wonder what it will feel like to achieve just one more thing and reach one more milestone. Christian writers are no different with all those feelings, but our solution to them may be different. We can offer our thanks to God, and rest assured that He loves us whether we are published or not.

We have learned that the writer's voice is, ultimately, a leadership voice. How you lead will very much depend on who you are. If who you are is rooted in relationship with Jesus Christ, you can be sure that you will lead faithfully and well. We can move and motivate readers to good things through our words. We can create beauty by writing excellent blogs and articles, letters and books, ad copy and speeches. We can—and maybe we should—delight for a while in what we create and in the impact of our words, even if their only impact is on our own souls. We are, after all, made in the image of our creative God. We honor Him when we steward well the passions and talents that He has given us.

But for all the excellent or beautiful words a Christian writer might write, we do well to remember that there is only one true Word. He made His dwelling among us, and He will one day return. His is the final and most lovely word of all. And for that, we are so thankful.

WHO WE ARE

Patricia Paddey is a freelance writer, editor, and communications consultant. Her writing has appeared in magazines and journals across North America and won numerous awards. She is a senior writer for *Faith Today* magazine. She co-authored *Shifting Stats Shaking the Church: 40 Canadian Churches Respond* (2015), *The Game Changers: True Stories About Saving Mothers & Babies in East Africa* (2016), and contributed to *Reflections for Advent* (published by World Vision Canada, 2016). Most recently, she co-wrote *Circle of Opportunity: Stories of Lives Changed Through Opportunity International Canada* (2019). With a background in broadcast journalism, she has written and produced segments and programs for both mainstream and faith-based Canadian television programs. She currently works part-time as Director of Communications at Wycliffe College at the University of Toronto. Patricia lives in Mississauga, Ontario and is pursuing a Master of Theological Studies part-time at McMaster Divinity College. She blogs at www.patriciapaddey.com

Karen Stiller is a freelance writer and editor. Her work has appeared in magazines and journals across North America. She is a senior editor of *Faith Today* magazine (Canada's Christian magazine), and the recipient of the A.C. Forrest Memorial Award from the Canadian Church Press for excellence in socially conscious religious journalism, among other writing awards. Stiller is co-author of two books about the Church: *Shifting Stats Shaking the Church: 40 Canadian Churches Respond* (2015), *Going Missional* (2012); and editor of *Evangelicals Around the World: a global handbook for the 20th century* (Thomas Nelson, 2015), and *The Lord's Prayer* (Wipf & Stock, 2015), by faculty at the University of Toronto (Wycliffe College). She has served as moderator of the Religion and Society series at the University of Toronto, a debate series between leading atheists and theologians. She has a Master of Fine Arts in Creative Non-Fiction from University of King's College and lives in Ottawa. Her spiritual memoir, *The Minister's Wife*, will be published by Tyndale House Publishing in Spring of 2020. www.karenstiller.com

ACKNOWLEDGEMENTS

We want to thank our husbands, Doug and Brent, who always encouraged us to write and to pursue our calling. Writers don't require cheerleaders, but they help. You guys are awesome.

Jenna Paddey happens to be related to one of us, but she is also a gifted artist, and we are thankful for her willingness to create the interior illustrations, which add a touch of whimsy and beauty to these pages. Find her at jpaddey.com or @jennapaddey on Instagram.

Writers need writers. We have both benefitted from being members of writing communities, sometimes even officially, like The Word Guild, an organization of writers and editors in Canada who are Christian. We both attended their conferences, participated in their online discussion groups, and strongly encourage writers to join associations like that one, especially at the beginning of your writing lives when it's easy to feel alone.

We'd like to express special thanks to Kristen Borgdorff and Belinda Burston—two writer friends of ours at opposite ends of their writing journeys (one a student and one now "retired") who read this book in its early stages and provided valuable feedback. We are grateful.

As we have matured in our writing and our lives, we do not find we need other writers less; in fact, we need them more. We depend on other writers to read and comment on our work, and also to share what they have been learning. We like to share our journeys with other writers. When we wanted to survey writers about their writing routines for this book, we turned to our writer friends on Facebook (of course). Thank you: Rikki, Sandra, Julie, Barrie, Susan, Robert, Alex, Carol, Brian, Myron, Marianne, Tim, Janice, Angelina, Lisa, Elma, Jan, Eric, William, David, Margaret, Amy, Janet, Patricia, Grace, Ruth, Dorene, Jennifer, Ann-Margret, Ron, Gwen, Preston, John, Ruth, Deb, Lynda, Rose, Charles, Marsha, Peter, Deborah, Marg, and Cassie. Thank you everyone!

AUTHORS AND WORKS CITED

We have been nurtured by the writings of other writers our entire lives, and we've quoted a cross section of some of our favorites in this book.

Buechner, Frederick. *Listening to Your Life: Daily Meditations with Frederick Buechner.* New York: HarperCollins, 1992.

Blundell, William E. *The Art and Craft of Feature Writing.* New York: Plume, 1988.

Craig, Mary. *Blessings.* London: Canterbury Press, 2012.

Dillard, Annie. *The Writing Life.* New York: HarperCollins, 1989.

Graham, Elaine, et al. *Theological Reflection: Methods.* London: SCM Press, 2005.

Hart, Jack. *Story Craft: The Complete Guide to Writing Narrative Nonfiction.* London: University of Chicago Press, 2011.

James, P.D. *Time to Be in Earnest: A Fragment of Autobiography.* London: Faber and Faber Ltd., 2010.

Karr, Mary. *The Art of Memoir.* New York: HarperCollins, 2015.

King, Stephen. *On Writing: A Memoir of the Craft.* Scribner. New York: Simon & Schuster, 2000.

Lamott, Anne. *Writing and Life: Some Instructions on Writing and Life.* Anchor Books. New York: Random House, 1995.

Lewis, C.S. *God in the Dock.* Grand Rapids: Wm. B. Eerdmans, 2014.

McEntyre, Marilyn Chandler. *Caring for Words in a Culture of Lies.*
Grand Rapids, MI: William B. Eerdmans, 2009.

McPhee, John. *Draft No.4: On The Writing Process.* New York: Farrar,
Straus and Giroux, 2017.

Merton, Thomas. *No Man is an Island.* Boston: Shambhala, 2005.

Newbigin, Lesslie. "Evangelism in the Context of Secularization." In
*The Study of Evangelism: Exploring a Missional Practice of the
Church,* edited by Paul W. Chilcote and Laceye C. Warner.
Grand Rapids: Eerdmans, 2008.

Nouwen, Henri. "Theological Ideas in Education" as quoted in *The
Christian Imagination: The Practice of Faith in Literature and
Writing,* edited by Leland Ryken. A Shaw Book. Colorado
Springs: WaterBrook Press, 2002.

O'Connor, Flannery. *Mystery and Manners: Occasional Prose,* edited
by Sally and Robert Fitzgerald. New York: Farrar, Straus &
Giroux, 2000.

Perrine, Laurence and Thomas R. Arp. *Sound and Sense: An
Introduction to Poetry.* 6th ed. New York: Harcourt Brace
Jovanovick, 1982.

Pipher, Mary. *Writing to Change the World: An Inspiring Guide
for Transforming the World with Words.* New York:
Riverhead, 2006.

Powers, William. *Hamlet's Blackberry: A Practical Philosophy for Building A Good Life in the Digital Age.* New York: HarperCollins, 2010.

Ryken, Leland. "Thinking Christianly About Literature" in *The Christian Imagination: The Practice of Faith in Literature and Writing,* edited by Leland Ryken. A Shaw Book. Colorado Springs: WaterBrook Press, 2002.

Sayers, Dorothy. *The Mind of the Maker.* New York: HarperCollins, 1987.

Shapiro, Dani. *Still Writing: The Perils and Pleasures of a Creative Life.* New York: Grove Press, 2013.

Shaw, George Bernard. Quoted in *Writing to Change the World: An Inspiring Guide for Transforming the World with Words,* by Mary Pipher. New York: Riverhead, 2006.

Shaw, Luci. Quoted in *The Christian Imagination: The Practice of Faith in Literature and Writing,* edited by Leland Ryken. A Shaw Book. Colorado Springs: WaterBrook Press, 2002.

Stein, Sol. *Stein on Writing.* New York: St. Martin's Griffin, 1995.

Willard, Dallas. Quoted in *Soul Keeping: Caring for the Most Important Part of You,* by John Ortberg. Grand Rapids: Zondervan, 2014.

Lightning Source UK Ltd.
Milton Keynes UK
UKHW011826190122
397399UK00003B/971